Danielle

TRIUMPH OVER TRAGEDY

BOBBY PETROCELLI
CHRIS FREDERICK

Brett

10
SECONDS

First published in the United States of America in 1995 by WRS Publishing, A division of WRS Group, Inc., 701 N. New Road, Waco, Texas 76710
Book design by Kenneth Turbeville
Jacket design by Joe James

10 9 8 7 6 5

Library of Congress Cataloging-in-Publication Data

Petrocelli, Bobby, 1960–
    Triumph over tragedy / Bobby Petrocelli, Chris Frederick.
      p.   cm.
    ISBN 1-56796-067-7 : $13.95
    1. Petrocelli, Bobby, 1960–   . 2. Christian biography--United States.
3. Coaches (Athletic)--United States--Biography. 4. High school teachers--United States--Biography. 5. Suffering--Religious aspects--Christianity.
6. Drunk driving--United States. 7. United States--Moral conditions.
I. Frederick, Chris. II. Title.
BR1725.P467A3   1995
248.8'6'092--dc20
    [B]   94-32348
                                                                CIP

DEDICATION

SUZANNE
For your immeasurable support

ALEC
For being who you are

MOM AND DAD
For laying a strong foundation in my life

TO MY FAMILY
For being there when I need you most

TO MY FRIENDS
For not having to be asked

TO THE HURTING OF THE WORLD
That you may find Faith, Hope and Love

IN LOVING MEMORY OF
Ava Lynn Dorsett Petrocelli

TABLE OF CONTENTS

A WIFE'S MESSAGE

People always ask me, "What do you think about your husband sharing his story?" I tell them that his message is a genuine story of triumph. It *needs* to be told. If he can make an impact on one life or can make someone else think twice before acting with poor judgment, he has done his job. Bobby uses words of courage and comfort, wisdom and love. Through sharing his own experiences of the joys and sorrows that make up life, he offers inspiration that hearts can be restored, despair can be turned to hope, and sorrow can become joy.

I would never have met Bobby if he had not gone through what he did. Not that I am pleased with what happened to him; if I could go back and change that pain, hurt, and devastation, I would. But I support and encourage him in sharing his message one hundred percent. Sometimes it is difficult to believe that Bobby has experienced such a terrible ordeal, because he lives each day to its fullest and never takes the gift of life for granted. Life is priceless, therefore, he tries to communicate to others how significant all decisions are.

Robert James Petrocelli is a man of courage, fervor, and immovable faith. Sometimes I think his name should have been Peter, which means "rock." He is a solid pillar of strength. As a husband and father, he shows this strength in every aspect of life. He may get up in front of an audience by himself, but when he speaks, both of us are really up there. I am deeply thankful for him. I love him, admire him, and will treasure him all the days of my being.

Suzanne Marie Petrocelli

ACKNOWLEDGMENTS

More than ever, I recognize the importance of relationships in our lives. This value became apparent to me during a tragic time. I received so much support through prayers, letters, flowers, visitations, and phone calls, an outpouring of the love of so many. It would take more pages than there are in this book to begin to thank everyone. Let me summarize by saying this:

Suzanne, I am truly the most blessed man in the world to have such an incredible wife. Alec, you are daddy's true "champ." To every awesome member of my family, you are simply the best. To the wonderful crew of "fellas" and friends, you have been sent. Chris Frederick, thank you for being a major part of this project. The list goes on and on.

And most of all, I thank you, God. "Without you I can do nothing." You have shown me what a privileged man I am.

If you were there for me in any way, your efforts have not gone unnoticed. The best part of it all is, *we are making a difference!*

FOREWORD

In a time when much of our world is in turmoil and most of the news is anything but good, Bobby's inspiring story of faith, courage, and love will touch your heart and remind us all that no matter how lonely, how dark how difficult circumstances may seem, we, too, can triumph over anything that may stand in our way.

He's a real-life "Rocky" and his story is a knockout!

Every young person in America should read this book so that they will know—without a doubt—the irreversible dangers of drinking and driving, and the unequaled importance of making good, responsible choices. And by the same token, every parent and adult should read this book so that they too will know how critical it is to establish and build strong foundations in our youth.

Each of us can make a difference, but we have to take the first step.

Bobby Petrocelli's life is now dedicated to bringing hope to all who will listen. He's an example to all of us—that we, too, can live a victorious and triumphant life.

Ann Jillian

PROLOGUE

AM I DREAMING?

Thursday. October 24, 1985. League City, Texas.

My wife Ava left that morning to go to work in Pasadena, Texas, a city south of Houston where she worked in the offices of a concrete plant. I left for my job in nearby Alta Loma, where I taught health education and coached at Santa Fe High School. Baseball and track I didn't mind so much, but the hours I put in during football season were long and grueling: seven days a week, August through November. In Texas, they live and breath high school football. For me it was my job, but for these Texans, football was their life.

I got home about 10:30 that night, which was normal during the season. Two of my greatest loves were waiting for me: my beloved wife, Ava, and a Jethro Bodine-size bowl of rigatoni. What more out of life do Italian men want than a loving wife and a jumbo bowl of pasta? Well, throw in "The Honeymooners," a second helping of pasta with homemade sauce, a few hours of sleep, and I'm rejuvenated for another day. Another day. Tomorrow. The sun always comes up tomorrow, right?

Of course.

After dinner, Ava and I settled into the living room, where she nestled into my lap to talk about the day's events and what was coming up with the approach of the holidays. Every night coming home from practice I anticipated holding Ava like this in my lap. It was such a simple pleasure, having my baby cuddle up to me each night and softly talk about her day.

One of the greatest feelings of being married is the intimacy, such as I had with Ava. It's funny to see big, hulking men melt like butter in the presence of the woman they love. I saw it in the other coaches and I saw it in myself—we melted like ice cream on the sidewalk on a hot July afternoon when our loves were nearby.

Ava and I had moved into a new house two months earlier, around Labor Day. It was a fresh start, with no more small apartments and no more small rooms. After two-and-a-half years of marriage, we were finally getting settled into the life we wanted. We couldn't have been happier.

Still wound up from the long day when we said goodnight and went to bed at 11:30, I tossed and turned for five minutes before getting up and stumbling my way through the dark into the kitchen for a glass of milk. I opened the refrigerator door. There was none. I was disappointed, since milk helped me sleep. It calmed me down. Instead, I had a glass of water. I came back to bed and asked Ava about the milk situation and she mumbled she would get a fresh gallon in the morning. She was a good wife. She knew what I liked, and I liked cereal, juice, and toast in the morning. I couldn't have asked for a better mate. I kissed her cheek goodnight, and we both fell asleep.

About an hour later I woke up. But instead of being in my bed, I was sitting in my dining-room window—one room away. I was confused. I was dazed. The smell of sulfur, tar, and burning rubber filled the room. Sulfur? Tar? Burning rubber? This dream was *vivid*. There was a stench about it, an unmistakable stench. I dropped my head for a moment, then picked it up and saw flickering lights coming through a foggy haze. Lights? Haze? The smell of tar and burning rubber grew stronger.

What a weird dream. What a weird feeling. I kept waiting to wake up. Somebody—wake me up.

I dropped my head a second time. When I looked up, there was a pickup truck in front of me. The smell. The stench. The lights. The truck.

A third time I dropped my head. Then I looked up quickly once again, trying desperately to shake myself out of this funk, this stupor I was in. Blue. The truck was blue and white. My bed was gone and there was a blue and white pickup truck in my house. I saw a man step out of the truck. He looked at me and I stared back at him. After an awkward moment of silence he said to me, "Is there anyone else in the house?"

What? Who is this man? What's this truck doing in my house?

"Is there somebody else in the house?"

I was silent as my brain went numb. Is there somebody else in the house? *Is there somebody else in the house?*

My wife. My wife! Where is my wife?

CHAPTER 1

BOY FROM BROOKLYN

Beepa shook me again, this time harder. "Time to get up," he said in his thick Swedish accent. "Bobby, it's *time* to get up."

My older sister Debbie and I used to mimic Nanny and Beepa's accent all the time. It was both funny and foreign to us. Beepa was from Sweden and Nanny was from Norway. They were our grandparents on my mother's side. My grandmother's real name was Gunhilde, and my grandfather's name was August Torsten. Gunhilde and August Torsten Carlson. To us, they were simply Nanny and Beepa. It was much easier that way.

Beepa had heard me screaming and rushed into the room to wake me up. "You ver screaming, Bobby. Are you all right now?" he asked with loving concern in his voice.

"Yes, Beepa. Where am I?"

Beepa hugged me. "You're at our house in de mountains, of course. Vhere did you think you ver? Don't you remember ve vent fishing today?" I sat in a sleepy stupor for a moment. I blinked my eyes and tried to shake the cobwebs out of my head. I was confused. This nightmare seemed real. It lingered vividly. Just then Nanny rushed into the room with a wet washcloth and a cold glass of water. No sooner had she stepped into the room than Beepa shot a sharp remark at her in Norwegian. Nanny snapped back as quick as a pistol. I didn't catch everything they said, but I knew it was about the spicy food I had had for dinner. Beepa made another biting comment, and Nanny hit him with the washcloth on the shoulder. This was how they squabbled. Nanny carried a mean washcloth. It was loaded and ready for another strike.

Beepa got wise and didn't say another word. "Ve're here, Bobby," Nanny said. "You're safe vith us now." Debbie

stormed into the room and said, "It's *time* to get up," in
Nanny and Beepa's accent. She could always make me laugh.
I looked outside and saw it was still dark. The lightning
bugs flickered beautifully in the night. Their lights flicked
on, then off, in the blackened night. I breathed in deeply
and filled my lungs with the crisp mountain air. I looked
out into the darkness and did it again. "What're you doin'?"
Debbie asked, puzzled.

Deep breath in. Release.

"What're you doin'?" Debbie asked again in a more critical tone. "Beepa got gas again?" she whispered to me.

"No," I said, laughing. "There was a certain smell that I
remember from my dream. It's not here now."

"Maybe that's why they call them dreams, Bobby, because they're not real," Debbie harped.

I half-laughed at her joking, but my nightmare this time
had been really scary. Debbie breathed in deeply. "The air's
a lot better here than in Brooklyn, I'll tell you that," she
said.

"Of course it is," said Nanny, "I'll take the Catskill Mountains over Brooklyn any day."

Beepa tucked me in bed and said, "Go to sleep now,
Bobby. Ve'll go svimming tomorrow."

"I love to *svim*," Debbie mimicked.

"You go to bed," Beepa barked, chastising Deb for making fun of his accent. I knew I couldn't look at Debbie or I
would burst out laughing. As soon as she was out the door,
I heard her laugh out loud. Beepa looked at me with a stern
look, then smiled and we laughed together. He brushed the
hair back from my forehead and patted me on the head.
"Tomorrow ve'll go svimming," he whispered, and winked
at me as he turned out the light and closed the door behind
him.

My father is Italian, with a little Brazilian mixed in. My
mother is Scandinavian, half Norwegian and half Swedish. I
came into this world on November 28, 1960, at Madison
Park Hospital in Brooklyn, New York, a good ol' American
mix of all of the above. I was the second of three children
born to Attilio Nunzio and Greta Carlson Petrocelli.

My father was no dummy. He married a blonde Scandinavian beauty. That's my pops. Attilio "Duke." Duke is what

his friends called him. He got the name as a boy because he was always fighting in the schoolyard. "Put up your dukes," he would tell the other boys. Almost everyone growing up in Brooklyn had a nickname. My dad's closest friends were Philly "Bumble" and Freddie "The Crow." Bumble got his name because he just looks like a "bumble," which is someone who is big, strong, hairy, and tough. Freddie got his when he came back to Brooklyn after the war with an army jacket with the name Crow sewn on it. You would've expected a more colorful story with a nickname like The Crow. Me? I was called "Pet" or "Petro." Short for Petrocelli. Anybody else in Brooklyn saddled with a normal name got a "y" tacked to its end. You know, like Bobby, or Joey, or Franky, or Suzy. Nicknames defined who you were.

My father was from a middle-class, blue-collar, Catholic background. He worked two jobs. His main job was with the New York City Transit Authority as a subway track foreman and inspector. He also worked part-time as a security guard at Madison Square Garden. A typical day for him was to work from early morning until four o'clock in the afternoon, come home, gobble down some dinner, and go to the Garden or to the stadium. During the summer months he worked at both Yankee and Shea stadiums.

My father worked hard for our family and helped me realize the importance of earning an honest living. "Bobby," he told me, "you can't brown-nose your way into anything. You have to work hard to achieve your goals. Don't ever be phony. Always be yourself. Don't try to be someone you're not. People can see right through it. But if you're honest and true to who you are, people will respect you for being a man, a real man." My mother would tell me, "Bobby, if you want to achieve things in life, you have to be willing to work hard. Then you can do anything you want to do."

My parent's hard work finally paid off—they achieved the American dream: to move out of our apartment on 24th Avenue and 86th Street in Bensonhurst, and move into our very own home on East 24th Street in Sheepshead Bay. It was an average middle-class home with two floors. My parents owned it and rented out the downstairs portion to another family. It had three bedrooms upstairs: my parents had one, my sisters, Debbie and Chrissy, had one, and I had the smallest one—in the front of the house facing the street. It didn't have air conditioning. I lay awake on summer

nights, unable to sleep because of the heat, and heard everything that went on in the street. I heard cat fights, beeping
horns, and couples arguing at all hours in the morning, and
saw teenagers roaming the streets. I saw it all. The best
thing that I saw from my window, though, were the people
in my neighborhood sitting out on the stoops in front of
their houses. They sat there for hours in their fold-out chairs,
drinking iced tea or another cold drink, just watching what
was happening in the street. And I was watching them watching what was happening in the street.

My mom was from a middle-class, Protestant, charismatic
Christian background. She worked an office job before my
sisters and I were born. Once she started the family, however, she felt that it was important to stay home and raise
the kids. But as we got older, she returned to work.

Both my parents worked hard to instill morals and values in our lives. They were disciplinarians. Certain things
were expected of us, and if we didn't obey, or if we answered back, we were in trouble. We were each responsible
for certain chores, whether it was running to the store,
taking out the garbage, shoveling snow, or cleaning up after
dinner. We knew what was expected of us.

When dinner was at 5:30, it did not mean we could
show up at 5:35. No straggling was allowed. We all ate
together as a family. As I look back, I'm glad we did. On the
afternoons when I was at the park and lost track of time,
out of nowhere I would hear my dad whistle the "Petrocelli
whistle." It was like a special call that meant, "You better
get your butt home for dinner right now, or you're not
going to have a butt to bring home for dinner no more." I
ran as fast as I could when I heard that whistle.

We all had assigned seats at the table: my father on my
left, my mom across from me nearest to the stove, Debbie
to my right, and Chrissy between my parents. Mom would
serve up macaroni, meatballs, Italian sausage, and a salad.
Before we ate, my father always said the same prayer. We
knew it so well that we mouthed the words as he repeated it
time and time again. He prayed, "Dear Jesus, bless the food
we are about to receive and thank you, thank you, thank
you, for blessing us and blessing our house. We thank you
in Jesus' name. Amen." We especially loved when he got to
the part, "and thank you, thank you, thank you... " There
was a rhythm to it, like a cadence. When he came to that

part, I would look at Debbie for the first thank-you, my mother for the second, and Chrissy for the third. Sometimes I changed the order.

After dinner my father would send us to get candy at the Pathmark Mini-Store, a five-and-dime store on Nostrand Avenue. "Bobby, run down to the store and get a Butterfinger, M&Ms, a couple of Mary Jane's, a Mounds, and an Almond Joy bar," he would say. That was our after-dinner treat. There wasn't a better way to top off a good meal than to have a candy bar from Pathmark. We loved them all. It's the little things like that I remember so well. I can still see my father lean back from the table, reach into his pocket, and hear the sound of change jingling around. He didn't have to say a word—we were already smiling before he said what he wanted. It was a magical sound, such a simple pleasure. Such a simple time. Time with your family goes so quickly, and once it is gone, you can never get it back. The years move on without our permission.

An old Jewish woman in her late sixties used to babysit us. Named Becky, she lived next door to us, so it wasn't a problem for her to come over and watch us once in a while when my parents wanted to have an evening out. Becky was sweet, but sometimes she had that musty, trunk-in-the-attic smell about her. Debbie would coax me to look up her dress or to make fun of her runny nose, and then when my parents came home she would be right by the door. "Bobby was making fun of Becky tonight. He was looking up her dress and laughing at her," she'd say.

When it came to being punished, my sisters and I did not get a choice like other kids in the neighborhood did. We were both spanked *and* grounded. A double whammy. It would have been nice to have one or the other, but not with *my* parents. I even remember begging them, "Please, just spank me, but don't make me stay in my room all day." I would have rather taken a little more spanking than get double punishment. But when it came to discipline, my parents did not play around. My father always made it clear to my sisters and me that he didn't want to ever hear that we had done anything to disgrace the Petrocelli name. We were never to embarrass the family. Discipline was important to my parents because it taught us respect. It also taught us that we were expected to do what was right, and if we made the wrong choice, there would be consequences to pay. We were responsible for our actions. This was one of the most important things my parents ever taught us—responsibility.

My sister Debbie is three and a half years older than I am. Chrissy is seven years younger than me. Because of the gap in age difference between Chrissy and I, we never had much in common growing up. When Chrissy was in first grade, I was in eighth and Debbie was in the eleventh grade. That was a huge difference at that time in our lives. As an adult, seven and ten years don't seem so much, but to a child time is different. Debbie and I found trouble together when we picked on Chrissy. One time we even tied her up with telephone wire and left her in the closet, then when my mother got home... Even so, I was still Chrissy's older brother. I took her to the park and out for ice cream. At the park, I'd tell the other kids, "This is my sister. You mess with her, you mess with me." When you're thirteen and your sister is six, it's easy to feel protective. I was a senior in high school when Chrissy was in fifth grade. As we've gotten older and become adults, we have grown much closer, and are now very active in each other's lives.

Both Christmas and Thanksgiving hold special memories. Our Thanksgiving table was always full. Besides the usual turkey and dressing, Nanny also cooked her special Norwegian dishes, which were incredible. We couldn't fit one more chair around that old wooden table of Nanny's. The meal was loud, full of energy, and exciting. I can still smell Nanny's homemade stuffing and almond green beans, the turkey with giblet gravy, and can taste the brown sugar on the sweet potatoes. I could never get enough of her cooking, and I often tried. Thanksgiving was more than a meal together—it was a celebration, an event, a gathering of the relatives to be thankful for the lives we had been given and our many blessings. It was a joyous time, when we felt a real freedom to laugh and enjoy each other's company. I can't imagine Thanksgiving any other way.

Most of my summers were spent at Nanny and Beepa's summer home in Lexington, New York, in the Catskill mountains, with my Uncle Artie and cousins Roy, Billy, and Allen. It was an experience my Brooklyn friends could only imagine. We swam in refreshing streams, jumping off ropes and bridges into the cool water below. We camped, fished, hiked, and explored ghost towns in the mountains. At least once a week we went to the drive-in movies. "It's my turn to sit in the back seat. You got to last time," I would tell my cousins, even though sometimes I had sat back there the time before. To sit out in the open air and watch a movie under the stars is something I'll never forget. There was something really cool about the little speaker that you'd hang in your window. The sound was terrible, but the fact that you had to hang the speaker on the car made it special—you knew you were at a drive-in movie! "There's a little man in that speaker," my father told us. "Where do you think the voice is coming from?" The fact was, we didn't know.

Getting fresh milk at the dairy farm was something we couldn't do in Brooklyn. Debbie and I would laugh and laugh at the smell of the barn. Somehow, the smell of manure gave us the giggles, and once we started laughing, we couldn't stop.

"Bobby, was that you? You stink," Debbie would say, holding her nose. "There's your twin right there," she would add as she pointed to the ugliest cow on the farm, slobbering and chewing on its cud.

"If that's my twin, then that's also your brother," I would snap back. Then she would chase me down and stuff hay down my back. If I was lucky, I would get her first—but she always made me pay later.

People don't believe me when I tell them I grew up on grits. Nanny cooked them almost every morning. And before we went to sleep at night, she would wash our feet. It must have been a custom she had brought with her from Norway. "Nanny, I'm ready," I would tell her each night, and then she would wash my feet, dry them, and tuck me into bed.

Many summers we piled into Uncle Artie's station wagon and drove across the country to visit my mother's brother in Washington state. Five different summers we traveled from New York to Loomis, Washington, to visit my mother's brother David and my cousins David, Danny, and Tania. Along the way we visited the Rocky Mountains, Mount Rushmore, San Francisco, Yosemite National Park, American Indian reservations, and the Smokey Mountains. I got to see a lot of country that many of my friends, most of whom spent their summers in Brooklyn, had never seen. The experience of traveling so much as a child gave me an appreciation for our beautiful country and the rich history, customs, and traditions of the different parts of the United States.

The Petrocellis have always stressed the importance of family. Two of my father's brothers, David and Vincent, lived near us in Sheepshead Bay, so I got to spend a lot of time with my cousins Mary Jo, Vinny (you should know by now that all true Italian families have a cousin Vinny), and Tony. Spending time at Uncle Davey's and Uncle Vinny's houses meant eating great Italian cooking. Aunt Dottie and Aunt Lucille cooked some unbelievable Italian dishes: stromboli, manicotti, calzone, you name it, they make my mouth water just thinking about it. Even now, during the holidays when I return to New York, I look forward to their cooking. My dad's oldest brother, Tony, lived in New Jersey. We saw them often because it wasn't far away.

The youngest of the Petrocelli brothers is my Uncle Rico, who lived outside Boston with my Aunt Elsie and their four sons. Uncle Rico, a professional baseball player, was a Boston Red Sox All-Star. He truly made the family proud. In 1961, after graduating from Sheepshead Bay High School in Brooklyn, he signed as a free agent. From 1965 to 1977 he played shortstop and third base for the Bosox. He helped lead the Red Sox to two World Series appearances—in 1967 against the St. Louis Cardinals and in 1975 against the Cincinnati Reds. Against the Cardinals he hit two home runs in one game. Twice he was named an American League All-Star, and in 1969 he hit forty home runs, which is still the American League record for most home runs by a shortstop.

Watching Uncle Rico play while I was growing up was exciting. You could always catch me following him on television or the radio, or in box scores in the newspaper. Uncle Rico will never know what kind of effect he had on my friends. When he did well, they were quiet and subdued. But when he had a bad game or wasn't playing well, they made fun of me. "Hey, Bobby—your Uncle Rico struck out last night with the bases loaded. What happened to him? Even I could've hit the ball somewhere," one would say.

"Oh, yeah," I'd say. "At least my uncle is a baseball player—not like yours, who works in the sewers."

The greatest thrill of all was going to New York's Yankee Stadium and Boston's Fenway Park to watch him play. I remember sitting in the dugout and locker room before the games, looking out onto the field, and thinking about great players from the past. I even had the privilege meeting the likes of Mickey Mantle, Joe Pepitone, Whitey Ford, Carl Yazstremski, Jim Lonborg, and Carlton Fisk.

One particular Saturday when I was six, I went to Yankee Stadium to watch my Uncle Rico play in an early afternoon game. It had been cloudy all morning. When I walked into the stadium—and I'll never forget this—the minute I stepped onto the field a beam of light lit up the right field bleachers. I looked up in the sky and the sun looked like a huge spotlight. It was as if someone had hit a switch and made the sun shine through, right on cue. The smell of the freshly cut green grass in the outfield was invigorating. I looked out at the magnificence of the place and stood motionless and awestruck.

My father's voice brought me back to earth when he said, "Bobby, come here for a minute." I walked backwards toward the dugout, still trying to take in the magnitude of Yankee Stadium and the echoes of greatness that I heard throughout the place. I felt myself getting near the dugout and when I turned, my dad said, "Bobby, I'd like you to meet Carl Yazstremski." Before I knew it, I was face to face and shaking hands with Carl Yazstremski. *The* Carl Yazstremski. *Yaz.* Then, in an instant, my dad was walking with Uncle Rico and escorting me to the Yankee dugout. Sitting right in front of me was Mickey Mantle. The Mick. He said, "Hi," and shook my hand as if I were a real person. Next I met Whitey Ford, the Yankees' pitching ace. I remember saying to myself, I hope someday I can play here and be just like Uncle Rico. He actually knew these guys on a first-name basis. I thought to myself, I don't care what my friends say about my Uncle Rico. Their uncles don't personally know Mickey Mantle or Carl Yazstremski or Joe Pepitone or Whitey Ford. They can laugh all they want. I hoped they had seen me on TV.

I was about seven when I got interested in athletics, especially baseball. With an uncle as a pro ballplayer and a father working at professional sports facilities, I developed a great love for the game. Not only did I watch Uncle Rico play, but Dad took me to stadiums when he worked. I saw the Yankees and Mets play all the time, with greats like Tom Seaver, Nolan Ryan, Reggie Jackson, Willie Mays, and

Hank Aaron. I watched the Knicks and Rangers play at Madison Square Garden.

From that time on I enjoyed competitive athletics. Most of my athletic talent was developed at a park one block from my house, where my friends and I played touch football, hardball on the concrete, basketball, and every form of stickball you can imagine. If we didn't go to the park, we played right in the middle of the street. We used manhole covers as the goal lines for football. The sidewalks were the out-of-bounds area. The telephone wires were our goal posts. Garbage pails (steel trash cans) were used for basketball hoops. We even played stickball in the middle of the street. Somebody's mother was always complaining about missing a broom handle, or two... or three... or four.

We played baseball in the street. We really didn't break too many windshields. Denting cars, now that was another story. "You kids go and play in front of your own house," Mrs. Wolfe, a neighbor, would yell down at us. Then she would hose down the street in front of her house so that it was too slick for us to play there. And we played hockey. We put on steel skates, the ones that fit over sneakers and had a key so you could tighten them.

During baseball season, I often got into arguments with my close friend Bruno. (Bruno's full name was Oreste Frank Bruno, but "Bruno" was his nickname. When you think of someone named Bruno, you probably think of a big, burly guy, six-foot-four and 250 pounds of muscle. Bruno didn't come close to fitting that description. He was short and skinny). We did everything together—played ball, went to school, joked around, hung out, threw snowballs at people from the top of his apartment building, you name it. One thing we did a lot was argue about which team was better, the Yankees or the Red Sox. Now you have to understand, Bruno was a big-time Yankee fan. I was a Red Sox fan. Our arguments got so heated that I'm surprised we remained best friends.

Playing ball in the streets, my friends and I emulated our favorite athletes. I would add my nickname to their already famous name. During football season I would be called "Joe Willie Pet" (Namath) and "O.J. Pet" (Simpson). Out in the street playing football, I would drop back to pass a long bomb to Bruno, announcing my own play-by-play: "Joe Willie Pet back to pass. He's being chased by Merlin Olsen.

He scrambles, breaks one tackle, Butkus is in hot pursuit. Joe Willie Pet sees Bruno in the end zone by Mrs. Wolfe's house. The street is dry and clear. Here's the pass. A perfect spiral towards Bruno all alone. *He caught it! Touchdown! What a great athletic effort from Petro. Harrrrrrrrr! Listen to that crowd, ladies and gentlemen."*

Eventually baseball became my number-one sport. I began dreaming of following in my uncle's footsteps. He had been a neighborhood hero. Everybody knew who he was—a local boy who "done good." I was starting to develop myself. Slowly, but surely, I began to hear the whispers. "That young Petrocelli boy ain't a bad ballplayer." Since I played at the same high school that Uncle Rico had, I was quickly gaining the reputation of being "Rico Petrocelli's nephew," but was making a name for myself as an outfielder. There wasn't a fly ball I didn't think I could chase down. Playing with future major leaguers like John Franco, I began to think about the possibility of someday playing pro ball.

Religion played another important part in my formative years. My parents felt it was essential that I attend church regularly from an early age and understand the importance of God playing an active role in my life.

Pastor Emanuel Greco, before he died, was a true role model. Not only was he the pastor of our church, but he had a family and was a New York City schoolteacher. He always showed me respect and love.

"Bobby, how're things going for you?" he would ask.

"Not too bad, Pastor."

"'Not too bad' can mean a lot of things, Bobby," he said, "'Not too bad' can mean 'they could be better,' or it can mean 'they could be worse.' Which one is it?"

He wanted you to be real and to cut through the bull. He was always interested in seeing what was really happening and would not just accept superficial responses. He was genuinely interested in people. That's why he was influential in my life, more than he would ever know. During my junior year at college, Pastor Greco sent me seven hundred dollars to help with tuition. His actions spoke as loudly as his words. He was a man of true integrity and genuine love for others.

Some of my closest friends were at our church: Joey Greco,

Vinny DeLuzio, and Jay Ferraro. Yes, we called each other by our regular names—not Joey "The Steeple" Greco, or Vinny "The Sanctuary" DeLuzio, or Jay "The Pulpit" Ferraro. We could be just who we were in church. Though we were from different parts of Brooklyn, we were all active together in our church group. It was kind of cool for me to talk to them and find out what was happening in other parts of the "Big Apple." We spent a lot of time together. We knew that we wanted God to be an integral part of our lives.

The four of us also spent time together outside of church. We rode bikes along the Belt Parkway up to the Verrazano Bridge, bowled together, went into Manhattan, or just hung out. I especially liked when the whole church group went out to eat. I guess after learning about faith you get hungry. Have you ever noticed that in many different religions, after going to temple or parish or church, everyone's ready to eat? And in New York we had places to eat. Boy, did we have places to eat! Any kind of food you wanted: Italian, Jewish, Chinese, German, Polish, whatever. It was so convenient—you could sit in the restaurant or get it to go. Potato knishes, calzones, White Castle hamburgers, submarine heroes, pizza. Food from every ethnic background.

My mother and father always emphasized work. When I was old enough, not only did I make a buck for myself, but I also gained a' true sense of responsibility and pride that comes with it. During my younger days, I looked forward to a snowstorm, going from door to door and making a couple of bucks for shoveling people's walks or driveways. In high school, the most memorable part-time job that I ever had was at Ruby's Luncheonette. It was a corner food establishment with a lunch counter and stools. Ruby's served sandwiches, soups, salads, and fountain drinks. They also served the most famous drink of all—the Egg Cream. Ruby's was known all over Brooklyn for making the best egg creams. (No, there aren't eggs in them.) There's a secret to a great egg cream. It takes milk, but the milk must be icy. Add chocolate syrup with a touch of vanilla syrup, stir in the seltzer water—and *viola*.

I worked as the clean-up crew, washing pots, pans, stoves, ovens, cleaning grills and windows. It was a rewarding feeling to work hard and bring home my minimum wage of

$2.10 an hour. There's something gratifying about doing an honest day's work. The work ethic established at Ruby's has always left me with the feeling of accomplishment and a job well done. There was a sense of pride attached to working for an establishment like Ruby's. Because he took pride in his work and his food, I could take pride in my work. I respected Ruby for working hard to make his place the best it could be and for the reputation he had as one of the best luncheonettes in all of Brooklyn. I was proud to tell people that I worked at Ruby's.

My parents also encouraged us to be independent and to experience as much of life as we could. My youth was filled with a number of diverse, positive experiences. My mother stressed the importance of working hard in everything that I did. She told me, "You can do anything that you want to do, be who you want to be, achieve your dreams and goals. But remember, anything in life that is worthwhile will take hard work and dedication." Those words echo in my heart now more than ever.

My parents tried to give me the best of everything, stressing to me the importance of family and faith, the need for integrity and honesty, and to always do the right thing. Always. To show respect and kindness to everyone.

The opportunity of growing up in the city and spending valuable time in the country gave me a well-rounded perspective for living life to the fullest. My parents instilled in me a sense of morals, values, and integrity that truly helped build a strong foundation in my life. With this foundation intact, I could face anything that would come my way.

CHAPTER 2

COLLEGE DAYS

Following outstanding baseball seasons at Sheepshead Bay, I opted to enroll in Oral Roberts University, a small NCAA Division I school in Tulsa, Oklahoma. I had liked ORU from an early age. Every Sunday morning I'd watch Oral Roberts' program on television while we got ready for church. I was drawn to the school by his compassion and genuine concern for others. I'd look at his beautiful campus on television and say, "That's where I want to go someday." I particularly liked that they emphasized physical fitness along with academics and spiritual growth. Besides that, the campus was spectacular on television. It looked like an exciting place to be. My mother supported and encouraged me in my choice.

Many of my peers coming out of high school played at St. John's and other powerhouse baseball programs on the East Coast. A few signed right away with pro teams and reported to their farm clubs, hoping to work their way up to the major leagues within a few years. I loved baseball, but I already knew that I wanted something more, something that baseball couldn't give. Something deep inside my heart.

Oral Roberts University is not for everybody. Plain and simple, it is a Christian institution with strict rules, excellence in academics, athletics, and spirituality. And unless you were there only to please your parents, you were willing to accept that certain behaviors were not tolerated. Those behaviors were defined by the Honor Code, which was spelled out clearly at the beginning of each school year.

The Honor Code was a document we were all required to sign. It listed a set of specific things that we would agree to do, or not to do. I can't remember anyone leaving for refusing to sign, yet many students signed knowing that they

would at one point or another break it. The Honor Code
established a sense of responsible conduct for the students.
We weren't supposed to drink alcohol, use drugs, have pre-
marital sex, cheat, plagiarize, copy, falsify, or be dishonest
or deceitful in any way.

The dress code called for men to wear a shirt and tie to
class, to Chapel, and to the cafeteria during specified hours
during the week. Women had to wear skirts or dresses during the same periods. But it wasn't as bad as it seems. The
general level of cleanliness and personal hygiene at ORU
was high. On the weekends, we dressed casually around
campus and could roll out of bed and into the cafeteria
with a mattress head and sweats on. But most of the time
we tried to look presentable. I respected that. I've had friends
in other schools who didn't have a dress code and it was a
completely different ball game. Some people today don't
care what they look like, but with such an emphasis on
appearance and image these days, more young people could
use this kind of dress code.

I arrived on campus in the fall of 1978 with my mother,
father, and Chrissy in our 1973 blue Chevy Impala. The
temperature was 107, and the Impala didn't have air conditioning. When my parents and sister left me at school and
started back to New York, I chased after the car, crying, as I
ran down the Avenue of Flags that led into the university. It
took some adjusting to get used to a small, relatively quiet
town like Tulsa after being from the "city that never sleeps."

Tulsa was hot in August. When you stepped outside, the
heat and humidity jumped on you. Stand outside for a few
minutes and in no time you'd drop twenty-five to thirty
pounds. I walked outside and the air was so hot that deep
breaths burned my throat and lungs. I quickly learned to
take shallow breaths.

After twelve hundred miles, I was here. In college. How
could I not be excited? The campus was straight out of *Star
Wars*. It was futuristic, shiny, and new. The buildings were
nothing short of spectacular. The mood on campus was
electric. It pulsated with an energy I can't explain. I guess it
happens on every college campus at the beginning of each
semester. There was an anticipation—an air of expectation.
As I walked across campus the first time, I saw new faces,

fresh faces, smiling faces. I wasn't used to people being so friendly and smiley. Big ol' smiles with white teeth. Not yellow, cigarette-stained, gap-toothed, nasty-teeth smiles like in Times Square. These people loved to smile. It was infectious, and the whole student body caught it.

But the biggest thing that struck me about the mood at ORU was a sincere, genuine feeling. People were happy to be there. People actually looked me in the eye. I wasn't used to that. Everybody said "Hello." One time while walking from one building to another I counted twenty-seven "hellos," eighteen "how's it goings," eleven "what's ups," five "howdys," three "nice to see ya's," and two "praise the Lords." They didn't have to yell at you to talk to you. You could have a civilized, person-to-person, no-holds-barred, quiet conversation. No horns blew, no taxis honked. Mrs. Corona wasn't yelling out the window for Mario and Nunzio to "come home for Spaghettios." You weren't worried about passing through another neighborhood and having somebody want to fight because you looked at them the wrong way.

The philosophy at ORU was simple: Help to make whole, healthy, complete, well-rounded people. Healthy in body, mind, and spirit. Years later, it's finally coming out that this so-called "new" philosophy of being healthy in every aspect of life is vital to the health of our fast-paced society.

Being an athlete, I appreciated the emphasis on physical fitness. As it was the late '70s, the aerobics program at ORU was well ahead of its time. The fitness craze hadn't yet caught on. The idea at Oral Roberts University was to encourage athletics and other related physical activities to the point that they would become not only a necessity, but also a natural part of students' lifestyles. I particularly liked the fact that so many of the women were serious about keeping in shape by running, doing aerobics, even swimming. Every guy knew that the girls looked great. Popular magazines, including *Playboy*, often rated our women among the best looking. We men at ORU quietly gloated about the accolades, even though it was officially against school policy to actually read *Playboy*. Since ORU was a religious institution, we had an honor code, or rather a set of moral standards to which we agreed to abide by while students. One of the rules was that we were forbidden to order and receive publications of this nature.

During my junior year someone wrote my name on a *Playboy* order card. When that first issue came to my box— the *only* issue to ever come to my mail slot—the mail lady was not amused.

"Young man, I don't know who you think you are, or what kind of background you come from, but we at Oral Roberts University do not and will not tolerate behavior like this. If you choose to continue to subscribe to this magazine, I will have you reported to the Dean of Men and recommend that he expel you from this school. Is that clear?" she asked.

"But, ma'am, I didn't subscribe to this magazine. Someone played a joke so I'd get in trouble," I pleaded.

"Do you boys think I'm stupid?" she said with her eyes narrowing and burning a hole straight through me.

"No, ma'am," I said.

"Fine. Then straighten up and fly right," she said as she closed the mailroom window, telling me that the conversation was now abruptly over.

Word spread quickly. Not word that I'd be expelled— who cares about that?—but word that *Playboy* had actually come. The guys on my wing had a field day. "Petro, I heard you got some *good* mail today!" one guy said with a big smile on his face. Another said, "Petro, I need some pictures for my anatomy presentation tomorrow! You got any I could borrow?" A third said, "Bobby, the dean called and wanted to know how our women rated this year. He's stopping by later to talk to you and also wants you to make an announcement in Chapel on Friday, okay?"

Can you imagine the university president standing up on the platform during the chapel service at a major Christian college—after twenty minutes of hymns, a scripture passage, and a seven-minute prayer—and saying, "I want to congratulate our female students' bodies—or rather the female student's body... Ahem, let me start again. I would like to congratulate our female student body for being rated No. 3 in *Playboy* magazine for having the third most beautiful women among universities in the U.S. We were only a few votes behind UCLA and Brigham Young, but we'll try harder next year, because, after all, isn't that what we're all about, being No. 1 in *Playboy* magazine?"

"*Haarrrrrrrrrr!*" responds the crowd, as the auditorium is whipped into a frenzy. After ten minutes, the celebration dies down just enough for the president to say, "Let's have the benediction, and don't forget to pick up your commemorative Issue from Bobby Petrocelli at the door as you leave." There is thunderous applause. "Okay, please, everybody. Bow your heads and pray with me. Our precious Heavenly... "

I thought that I was going to be kicked out of school for something I didn't do. They were brutal on me. I had been set up. Big time. It wasn't that funny then, but I can laugh about it now. And I know exactly who sent it to me too. Cheeks, my half Filipino friend.

Going away to school was one of the best things I ever did. I was away from my parents, away from my neighborhood—away from the safety and "comfort-zone" I had known in my familiar surroundings. It forced me to become independent. This is how I grew. This is how I learned. This is how I matured.

Sometimes I felt as if I were the only freshman on the whole campus. I often strode confidently through the campus completely lost because I wanted to look as if I knew where I was going. Soon, though, the Law of Magnetic Ignorance kicked in. That's the Unexplainable Phenomenon that happens when two lost freshmen attract each other, then a third, and a fourth, and soon there's a pack, and then a mob, growing, feeding, searching, stuck together by class rank and ignorance. They roam together likes wolves, desperate to be accepted into the pack. The pack of ignorant freshmen.

Registration Day. August 1978.

"Where's the CC?" I sheepishly asked a guy, looking for the Classroom Center.

"You a freshman?" he said back at me with a little bit of an attitude.

I hesitated. "Yeah..." I felt like saying, "Yo, you got a problem with that?" but I didn't. The truth was, I *was* a freshman. I found out later that he was, too. He just said it in such a demeaning tone that I wouldn't have ever known.

Following his directions, I walked past the cafeteria and approached a white-domed building. As I got closer, I heard the noise inside getting stronger and louder. "Somebody's having a party here," I thought. I opened the door and stepped inside. It was nothing short of walking into the pit of the New York Stock Exchange. Registration. It was wild. Students frantically ran from one line to the next. I had absolutely no idea where to start. I surveyed the area and felt dizzy for a moment.

Finally, the Law of Magnetic Ignorance caught me and swept me to one side of the room where a sign read, "Start here." God must've had pity on me because I ended up in the right line. "Last name?" the woman behind the desk asked me.

"Petrocelli," I said.

She searched through the "P" section and pulled out a card with my name on it. "Robert J. Petrocelli?" she asked in a serious tone.

"Yes, ma'am," I replied in a little stronger voice this time.

"From Brooklyn, New York?" she asked.

"Yes, ma'am," I acknowledged.

She smiled as she handed me the card. It was a peculiar kind of smile, as if she knew something that I didn't. Like she was saying, "You should be used to this craziness. You should feel right at home in this atmosphere." You know something? As stupid as this may seem, I did. It was the first thing to happen that reminded me of home. At that instant I grew about a foot taller, or rather my confidence did.

Freshmen registered last. By the time it was our turn after the seniors, juniors, and sophomores, we had to settle for whatever we could get. It was a rat race. Students ran from line to line, trying to secure certain classes before they filled up. No one liked to get up on Monday morning and no one liked to be stuck in class on Friday afternoons. I registered for the 7:50 a.m. classes since these were the classes nobody wanted. I didn't mind, though. I like getting up early and don't mind early morning classes. I never could lie in bed all day. I'm an early bird. It's in my nature to be driven and to get things done. I didn't find many other students who thought quite the same way.

Studies didn't come easy at ORU, but I learned *how* to study. My freshman year was my weakest, and I managed to reach just below a "B" average. I improved my sophomore year and pulled my grades up every year after that. ORU was not the type of school that you could do nothing and expect to pass classes. Even the general education classes that everyone had to take were tough. There were no freebies. None. Zip. *Notta.*

ORU definitely wasn't a party school. Professors took attendance in every class, and cutting class dropped your grade. A lot of students complained about the attendance policy, but I'm glad ORU had it. It showed the administration cared that we got the best education possible. Some of my friends at state schools laughed when I told them about the attendance policy, but they weren't in school to learn. They were there to have a good time. "That's what college is for," they said. "Party time." Hey, I had a great time in college. It all depends on the people with whom you associate. You choose your own friends. You have to make sure you choose them well.

The friends I made at ORU are still my best friends today. We lived together, laughed together, pretended to study together, ate together, played together, prayed together, worked together, struggled financially together... You get the picture.

I knew from the start of my sophomore year that I wanted to be a teacher and coach, so I declared health and physical education as my major. I had never had a coach whom I really looked up to or admired, and I wanted to be the coach I had never had. I loved the physical education classes, but the toughest ones were the health and science courses. They were *work.* Anatomy and physiology were monsters. Pre-med majors and nursing students definitely had my sympathy. If that's what they wanted to do, God bless them. I'd gladly coach their children.

I was fortunate to live with guys who had it all: athleticism, good looks, brains, and a love of God. Most of all, they knew how to have a good time. We had a lot of good times. Not the kind that you think you enjoy while you're doing it, like getting drunk out of your mind, and then not being able to remember what you did. I'm talking about memorable, funny, off-the-wall things that I still laugh about now, years later. The memories are still vivid in my mind, as if they had happened just yesterday—memories and friendships that I wouldn't trade for anything in the world.

Jay Ferraro was one of those friends. I called him "House"

because he was a massive guy, a huge bodybuilder. I knew
Jay through church back in Brooklyn, and he came to ORU
because of my description of the school. We roomed together my junior and senior years. Jay was studious and
disciplined, probably from his weight-training work ethic.
Craig Olson was another buddy I met when I first started
school. He was a good athlete, had a great sense of humor,
and was a good student. Craig was in charge of hiring per-
sonnel for seminars that the university hosted, and managed
to get me a lot of campus jobs.

Dave "Riv" Rivera was my resident advisor. Riv was from
Spanish Harlem and had attended the school of music and
art on which they based the television show "Fame." Riv
looked like a Latin lover-type, but he wasn't. He was cool
and used to drive the girls crazy with his slow, sleepy eyes.
John "Jakey" Jones is the only guy I know who gave himself
his own nickname. He came into school as a freshman with
Jay and Cheeks in 1980, my junior year. Jakey was from
North Carolina and, to this day, won't admit that he wore
cowboy boots and a leather belt with his name on it. Jakey
was deceptively smart. He also had a way of charming the
girls and we joked with him about "lipping up" on too
many. Joe Liberatore came out of high school as one of the
most heralded baseball players in Indiana. He and Don
Mattingly of the New York Yankees were among the top
players in the state. Joe was recruited by ORU and played
outfield for the Titans. I still joke with him about hitting a
Roger Clemens fastball off of the centerfield fence in a game
against the University of Texas. Joe and I became close while
we were teammates on the baseball team.

Cheeks was another good friend at ORU. Half-Filipino,
he came from inner-city Pittsburgh. He was always laughing
and joking and messing around. He was either just messing
around, or playing basketball and messing around. He, along
with my other buddies, were the type of guy who would do
anything for you. They would give you the shirt off their
back. Most people are lucky to have one friend like that. I
had many of them.

When I think about them now, I realize we did some
crazy things in school. Nothing really to hurt anyone, but
off-the-wall, funny, mischievous things. If it happened to
be your birthday, we might jump you in the room, strip
you naked, tie your hands and feet, put you in a fold-up

rollaway bed, and close the bed with your feet hanging out one end and your chest and head hanging out the other. Then we'd wheel you over in front of one of the women's dorms and park you there with a big red ribbon tied around the bed and sing a rousing rendition of "Happy Birthday" to you. You were on your own to get back to the dorm unless you could convince an innocent female bystander to help you, but we strongly discouraged any good Samaritans for at least ten or fifteen minutes. After that, we were as helpful as can be. Especially with summoning help. We would shout, "Come on, girls. Who wants to help the birthday boy?" By that time you wished that it wasn't your birthday anymore. And you were wishing you had more clothes on than just your birthday suit.

We also had wing wars, when one wing of the dorm declared war on another. These were anything from shaving-cream battles to water fights. During one massive water fight with a wing downstairs, our wing drenched their entire floor and soaked most of their rooms. When the downstairs wing tried to retaliate, they made a tactical error by coming up the elevator. As soon as the elevator door opened, everyone inside was deluged with a typhoon of water. Wave after wave, we hit them until an inch of water stood on the floor. The poor guys kept hitting the button for the door to close, but what they didn't know was that we had put a piece of duct tape over the button on the hallway elevator button, so there was absolutely no way to close the door. When they finally realized what we had done, it was much too late. Poor guys, I heard they didn't dry out for a week. They never attacked us again.

During winters, ice and sleeting rainstorms are usual for Oklahoma, but accumulating snow is more rare. When it did come down, classes were canceled, and we went sledding on cafeteria trays and had brutal snowball fights. These snowball fights were greatly discouraged because someone was always getting hurt or hit in the eye, but we loved them. The best one we ever had was in January 1982. It had snowed all afternoon and the snow was perfect for snowballs. The temperature wasn't too cold, around twenty-nine or thirty degrees, and it was a wet snow. The snowballs packed easily and they packed well. It started off rather innocently in front of the cafeteria, where a few guys from Towers dorms started throwing at guys from EMR, my dorm.

As more and more guys came out of the cafeteria and joined in, however, the action started to heat up. Guys weren't just out to hit someone, they were out to "tattoo" one another, all in the name of pride for the dorm in which they lived. I compare it with the pride you feel in being from a certain neighborhood or city.

I was with Jay, Jakey, and Cheeks when we came out of the cafeteria and saw what was happening. Jay said, "Look, it's a snowball fight!" By the time he got to the word "snowball," Jakey and Cheeks were already down the steps, across the sidewalk and had three snowballs each in their hands. Jay and I quickly followed and ran across the same sidewalk and into the parking lot where the battle was starting to take shape.

Jakey and Cheeks were crazy. That's all you need to know about them. They just wanted to hit somebody. I saw them hit about five guys with snowballs before they realized their targets were from our own dorm. By this time, the snowball fight had grown to about ten against ten, with more joining in. The parking lot was a perfect battlefield. There was plenty of fresh snow on the ground and on the cars, and you could use the vehicles as shields while reloading ammunition.

"Petro, look out!" Cheeks yelled as I got hit in the leg with an iceball.

"Owww," I said. It stung, and that's what got me into the game. Jay, Jakey, Cheeks and I alternated making and flipping snowballs to each other to maximize our firepower. The EMR guys made a surge and began pushing the Towers boys across the parking lot toward the Towers dorm. Both forces had grown to about fifty men each. We kept firing and ducking, firing and ducking, preparing to advance in a massive wave of fury.

"You ready to go, Jay?" I yelled.

"Let's do it, Bobby," Jay darted back at me.

I peered over the snow-covered Jeep that I had been ducking behind and saw a continuous array of white iceball-like missiles flying through the air in every direction.

"Pet, we hit seven guys each already, and you're still making your ammo," Jakey jabbed at me.

"Yeah, but five of those guys were from *our* dorm," I yelled back.

Jakey just smiled a toothy smile to let me know he didn't care who he hit. Cheeks stood up and fired four snowballs in a row. Three hit one guy in the back. "I lit him up! Battin' seven-fifty!"

Cheeks and Jakey were getting into this a little too much, acting like Marines spearheading frontal assaults. A snowball whizzed by my head.

"Let's *go!*" Cheeks yelled as he led another surge. Jay and I grabbed four snowballs each and sprinted about twenty-five yards to the front line where Jakey and Cheeks were. Thirty guys followed as we started to drive the Towers boys up the hill toward their dorm. When the rest of our guys saw the wall pushing them back, they all joined in. We bombarded them continuously and mercilessly. We had them pinned in and they had absolutely nowhere to run and no way to escape. It was like a firing squad as guys got hit with two and three snowballs at a time.

All at once we heard whistles blow down in the parking lot behind us. Five campus security guards ran confidently across the parking lot in formation, blowing their whistles at us to stop. They reached the edge of the parking lot, which was directly below the hill on which we were standing. The leader of the fivesome said matter-of-factly through a megaphone, "You men are asked to disperse quietly. Snowball fights are against university policy and you must stop throwing them immediately. If you do not disperse quietly and return to your dorms in an orderly fashion, we will be forced to take punitive actions against you."

Mistake No. 1: There were only five of them. Mistake No. 2: They didn't know what kind of minds they were dealing with. Mistake No. 3: They were standing at the bottom of the hill. You get the picture.

We stood looking down at them. An eerie twenty seconds of silence passed. Again the leader spoke, more harshly into the megaphone this time, "I am *ordering* you to disperse and return to your dorms quietly," he barked. Another fifteen seconds of tense silence filled the air.

Then it happened. As if it had been choreographed and practiced beforehand, all one hundred guys on that hill stepped forward into one straight line across the top. We saw what was coming. It was the O.K. Corral, and somebody was about to not be O.K. The security guards saw what was coming. I saw the disbelief in their eyes. The silence screamed for a solution.

Cheeks and Jakey started laughing, a maniacal, diabolical, sinister laugh. One hundred and five men knew exactly what was about to take place, but five of them were on the wrong side, and at the bottom of the hill. Jakey let out an Apache Indian yell and, all together, every man on that hill yelled, then rained a barrage of snowballs down on those five poor security guards. We pummeled them. When the barrage came to an abrupt halt, chaos ensued as everyone sprinted for their dorms. It was now every man for himself. The guards tried to grab whomever they could. A sea of refugees poured into EMR's lobby, all of us with our adrenaline pumping and slapping each other high fives for making it back safely. It was a feeling I'll never forget. Jay, Jakey, Cheeks and I laughed for fifteen minutes. I was glad to be a part of it, just another one of too many crazy predicaments that I got into with Jay, Jakey, and Cheeks.

I'll never forget when Cheeks and Jakey "borrowed" a campus security golf cart. They came riding up to the baseball field after practice in the cart they had stolen from in front of the security building. They offered me a ride to the gym and I climbed aboard.

"Where'd you guys get this cart?" I asked, thinking I already knew.

"At the Honda dealer on 67th and Harvard," Cheeks said.

Jakey laughed. "Cheeks, don't lie to Petro. We got it from the Pontiac Dealer on 31st and Sheridan."

"You guys are some sick puppies," I chuckled.

"Don't forget to tip your drivers," quipped Cheeks.

Unbeknownst to me, campus security guards were combing the campus in other carts looking for them. Thirty seconds after they dropped me off at the gym entrance, I saw the abandoned security golf cart rolling by itself down the sidewalk at the bottom of the hill. Jakey and Cheeks ran frantically by me into the gym, guards in hot pursuit. "Hey, come back here, you two!" the guards yelled. Jakey and Cheeks never got caught. Figures.

I tried out for the varsity baseball team my freshman year and was cut after several months of workouts. I was especially disappointed because I could have gone to many other colleges and played, but ORU was a national collegiate power and was in the Top 20 year in and year out. Mike Moore, our ace pitcher, was eventually drafted by the

Seattle Mariners in the 1981 draft. He was not only a first-round draft choice, but was the first player taken overall. Of anybody!

I worked hard getting in shape the summer before my second year in school as I prepared to try out for the Titans again. Larry Cochell, the head coach, heard that I was Rico Petrocelli's nephew and wanted to see what I could do. He worked with me, but I didn't make the final cut. I was close. I was *this* close. At least I made an impression on him. That made me feel better. Still, any athlete is not satisfied with almost doing something. They have to *do* it.

The next summer I was determined to come back faster, stronger, and with a better batting stroke. At six feet, two inches and 159 pounds, I felt small compared to the other players on the team, but I worked hard all summer in Brooklyn and felt that this was my time to shine.

It was a gorgeous late August day in Brooklyn when I tore up my ankle. The days were still warm, but the nights were cooling down. A great time of the year, just days before heading back to school for the fall semester, I was just about to finish up a good thirty-minute bike ride. My legs felt strong. They were tired, but it was a good tired. I was cooling down and heading for the homestretch of my ride, just a few blocks from my house, when I rode too close to a curb. My pedal caught and pulled my ankle under with it. Down I went. Ligaments tore.

I was devastated. I had worked all summer long, determined to make the Titans. I wanted to make my father and Uncle Rico proud. Now, after a stupid bicycle accident, I could hardly walk, let alone be in any condition to make the team.

On the floor of the ORU's basketball arena are the words "Expect a Miracle." I knew that if I were to make the team now, I would truly have to believe in a miracle. I believed in that phrase. I needed a miracle desperately. Back at school during the tryout, some friends came to the stadium to encourage me on. I knew I would have to put the adversity behind me and think about the goal I wanted to achieve. My defense and my arm strength have always been solid, but hitting is what makes or breaks you in baseball. I stepped up to the plate for the first pitch from Jim Brewer, the assistant coach who used to pitch for the Dodgers. All I wanted to do was to make good contact with the ball each time.

The first pitch screamed by. It was a perfect strike. I saw it go by right down the pipe. I stepped out of the box and dug my feet in to get comfortable. The next pitch came in and I fouled it off, hard down the first base line.

"I'm swinging late," I said to myself. "Get this pitch, now. Get this pitch." The next four pitches I hit hard for clean base hits. I felt good about it. I got into a groove and the bat felt sweet and smooth. Coach Cochell took a liking to me and saw potential in me as a player. My hard work had, in fact, paid off, as I made the team both my junior and senior years. I was a Titan. I had done it, but not without a fight. We were again ranked in the Top 20 both years that I played, and just missed going to the College World Series. Part of the season we were ranked No. 1 in the nation. Oklahoma State beat us by one run, two years in a row. They were bitter defeats, especially because there was such an intense rivalry between the two schools. Nonetheless, it was a tremendous experience to play with and against some of the guys that I did. Roger Clemens of the Red Sox was pitching for Texas, along with Spike Owen. Kevin McReynolds, now with the New York Mets, played at the University of Arkansas.

J.L. Johnson Stadium, our ballpark, was one of the most beautiful college fields in the country. I remember how proud I was at being able to put on the uniform and play in such a great facility. It was a tremendous opportunity, but I was used sparingly as a substitute outfielder. I had excellent speed and a good arm, but for some reason I couldn't hit the curveball. I joke about it today that there were only three things keeping me from a lucrative pro career: Fouled off the fast ball, fouled off the change-up, but couldn't touch the curveball.

All four years at ORU I lived in the "middle-class" dorm, E.M. Roberts Hall. Nine hundred guys lived there, about thirty-six on each wing. They were all regular, down-to-earth guys from all over the country, and even international students from Kenya, Hong Kong, Canada, Nigeria, Iran—everywhere. The richer, preppy students lived in the Towers, which were nicer and cost more. There definitely was a separation of classes. I could have lived with the athletes in the athletic dorm, but I decided I'd rather stay in EMR. One thing I did take advantage of was eating at the AD. They had their own cafeteria and the food was better than in the main cafeteria.

Every Monday night at 11 p.m. every floor on campus had a mandatory "wing meeting." All thirty-six guys sat out in the hall together on the floor and the resident advisor made announcements, gave sports results from intramurals, scheduled events, sister wing activities, and so on. It was a great time to get together and sit around and laugh and joke. Wing meetings were supposed to last about twenty minutes, but we had so much fun that we'd often go on for thirty or forty-five minutes. The term now used to describe what happened at wing meetings is "male bonding," but it was actually more than that. These were good, solid guys, a bunch of guys who really cared about each other and how each one felt. The feeling was sincere and it was genuine. It transcended where we were raised and where we came from. We knew where we were going. We were headed for the same goal—a much higher goal.

All thirty-six of us sat on the floor of our long hallway on our Youngblood Wing. Riv took a moment to count heads. "Who's missing? Anybody?"

"We're all here, Riv," Dietmar Krein said.

"All right, let's get started with a word of prayer. 'Dear Father God, we thank you for this group of men on Youngblood. We ask that you would be in our midst now as we talk and fellowship together. Go before us in all we do this week—in our studies and what we do for you. Help us to glorify you in what we say and do. In Christ's name. Amen.'"

Everybody echoed, "Amen."

"Now the first thing we have to talk about is that this week is Secret Sister week," Riv said.

A voice from the back said, "I don't have any money. I'd hate to have me for a secret brother, poor as I am."

"Do like Petro did last year and give her a can of string beans one day, and a can of baked beans the next day!" another voice proclaimed.

Everybody laughed. "And, Pet, don't sign 'Love, your Secret Brother—Bobby Petrocelli' this time, either," another voice chimed. There was a huge roar this time. It was one of those moments that we laughed because it was funny—and we laughed because it was true. The previous year I had given a signed card on the second night, "Love, Your Secret Brother—Bobby Petrocelli."

The phone rang in someone's room. "That's the sisters calling to say, 'No green or baked beans this year, please!'"

Everybody was always cutting up and joking all the time. The one time during the wing meeting that we never joked around was during prayer. We sincerely lifted each other up in prayer concerning anything that someone wanted to share with the group. This was the best time of the meeting, because guys would just open up their hearts and speak freely and honestly about family concerns or prayer requests. Yeah, we knew how to joke, but we also knew how to care for each other enough to pray for one another.

I look back now and it's amazing to me how it was planned out. There's no doubt in my mind that every step of the way of my being at ORU was part of a larger, complex, yet complete plan that was being orchestrated for me, from the guys I met on my wing, to my making the baseball team—even after the bicycle accident. It was as if a blueprint for action were already in motion on my behalf.

CHAPTER 3

TEXAS BELLE

I met Ava at the beginning of my senior year. She was standing on the steps of the cafeteria talking with Jay and her best friend Toni Swain, whom Jay was dating. Toni was a tow-headed blonde, the type of girl who turned heads when she entered the room, but my head turned toward Ava. Ava had beautiful, long brown hair, an angelic face, and dimples that deepened when she smiled. I acted like I always did when I met an attractive girl for the first time— excited, constantly smiling or trying to suppress the smile on my face, and trying to come across as a pleasant guy with a good sense of humor.

"Hey, Bobby," Jay said. "I'd like you to meet Toni's friend, Ava Dorsett."

"Hi, Bobby, it's nice to meet you," she said in a soft Texas accent that made my name sound gently like *Bawby*. "Jay has talked a lot about you."

"Don't believe a word he says. I'm not Travolta's brother," I joked. She smiled and gave a cute little giggle.

She got the joke, I thought to myself. This was good. Sometimes a girl I joked with thought I was serious and I'd feel stupid. But Ava got it. A good sense of humor, I thought.

"Jay says you're a P.E. major?"

"Yes. Health and phys-ed. I'd like to coach."

"Oh, really?" she said. "My parents are both former physical education teachers. They loved it."

We talked about ten minutes more. I found out that her parents were not only former P.E. teachers, but coaches as well. Ava's father had gone to the University of Houston and played in the NFL for the Oakland Raiders and the Houston Oilers.

Our relationship was not a "love at first sight" type of thing, but we spent time together with Jay and Toni and gradually developed a friendship that deepened as the days went by. During the first three months we got to know each other through going out in groups or with other couples. Jay, Toni, Ava, and I spent a lot of time together. The four of us ate together, studied together, and went to the movies together. Mazzio's Pizza was a popular gathering spot for the four of us.

I liked Ava because she was fun to be with and because she liked a lot of the same things that I did. We took study breaks, usually twenty minutes or so, and read the Bible together. We worked in community outreach programs together. We had a compatibility, a kind of chemistry. I felt comfortable with her and, above all, I felt a freedom to be myself.

That's something that I would always look for in a woman: if she was cool in letting me be myself. "Hiya, toots," I'd say in my high-pitched Curly voice from "The Three Stooges." "Oh, a wise guy, eh? I'll show you. Ladee ladoo, nyuck nyuck nyuck, whoop oop oop oop oop." I continued through the whole routine. I like to joke around and be silly and goofy sometimes. Other times I like to be serious. I just wanted to be able to be real with whomever I dated. That was important to me. That's something young people should look for: someone they can be themselves with and not feel as if they have to be something they're not.

I'll never forget the time that Jay, Toni, Ava, and I spent the entire day at Keystone State Park, outside of Tulsa. It was a beautiful park with a big lake and trees all around, a place to take a welcome break from being around school on a Saturday. It was a gorgeous day—sunny, warm, and with blue skies. The water on Lake Keystone was a deep, rich, royal blue. There was a crispness in the air, a bite. Clean and refreshing like a spring day. It was one of those magical days that you wish you could bottle up and bring out whenever you want to. They only happen about once a year and you have to make sure you take advantage of them when the opportunity arises.

I remember days like this growing up, at Nanny and Beepa's house in the mountains. Always in the summertime, though. Late summer. August. The morning would be cool and breezy, then by midday it would be warm enough to swim. And at night just after the sun went down, the crickets would sing. Nanny would make sure we put on a sweater if we went outside in the cool night air. This was a Nanny and Beepa night. "*Bob*-by, come *here*. Put dis sveater on, it's chilly outside," Nanny would say, right before she broke into Norwegian, playfully scolding Beepa for not getting a sweater for me himself.

I can still smell that musty old sweater and the scent of the woods, and the unmistakable fragrance of pine all around me. Every once in a while I'll get that feeling of *dejà vu*—a certain aroma, a familiar face, or just something that reminds me of something from the past. I like when that happens. It touches places in my heart that I thought I had forgotten. I like to remember. I miss Nanny and Beepa. I also miss going to the mountains. Places from a more innocent, simple, unsophisticated time.

That night at the lake, after three months of friendship, I finally decided that Ava was someone with whom I'd like to have a more serious relationship. I had met Ava for the first time around the last week of August, and it was now October. As hard as it may be to believe, I was about to kiss her for the very first time. I was old-fashioned that way.

The sun had set about an hour and a half earlier. It was a spectacular setting—long, warm, full of reds, oranges, and yellows. We sat there for the entire eleven minutes that it took the sun to completely fade from the sky. The silhouettes of the trees all around the park were mysterious and spooky, yet there was a natural, haunting beauty that enveloped us for a half hour more as the light faded into the darkness of night. It had been another wonderful touch to an already terrific and memorable day. But the night was still young, and there was romance in the air.

"Today has been as close to perfect as I could ever ask for," Ava said softly, in her slight Texan accent.

"Yep," I said, "we picked an awesome day to come out here."

We had made a fire and the embers were glowing an almost inviting orange-red. There's something mesmerizing about staring into the glowing coals and embers of a fire. You look at them and stare, almost as if you're in a stupor, captured in their trance-like power. The crickets had begun their songs, the fireflies were dancing an enchanting ballet of lights around us, and the crackle of the wood in the fire was the only thing that brought me out of my sleep-like stare. I don't know if this is true for everyone, but for me it is: I'd get to the point in a relationship in which we hadn't yet kissed, and know I was facing the moment of truth. It could be a couple weeks, a month or, in this case, three months.

Over the last few weeks I had gotten comfortable with Ava and was wondering when the right time would be—the right time to kiss her for the first time. She sighed a heavy sigh as we both were transfixed by the amber coals in the fire. She shifted her position and snuggled closer to me, so that we were touching side-to-side, shoulder-to-shoulder, hip-to-hip. She leaned into me and rested her head on my shoulder. I looked over at her and she smiled that patented Ava smile, the one where her top lip got thin, she showed her perfect white teeth, and her dimples deepened on her cheeks.

I looked at her smile, then looked into her eyes. I could feel my heart start to beat faster and I breathed short, awkward breaths of air. She reached over and touched the back of my hand with hers and I got goose-bumps in an instant. We both looked in each other's eyes and started to lean in toward one another's space. Slowly, slowly, we merged—and melted into each other's "personal space" zones, that intimate space that we only let a few selected people in our lifetime into. I saw her eyes close right before I closed mine, and then felt her soft, moist lips lock with mine. The first touch turned into a deep, meaningful, passionate kiss, one I'll never forget. My first one with Ava, that October night in Keystone State Park near Tulsa, Oklahoma. Today, a lot of people consider it an insult to *not* get a kiss on the first date. Some people expect more.

This was the beginning of what I hoped would be a long and deepening relationship. Over the next several months, I found out that Ava wanted this as much as I did—a long and deepening relationship.

During Christmas break in 1981, Ava asked me if I wanted to fly down to Friendswood, Texas, near Houston, to meet her family. Usually when you get to the point of meeting someone's family—especially if she's flying you down from New York to Texas—you think something is happening.

Something *was* happening. For the first time, my parents saw that I was serious about this girl being the one with whom I wanted to spend my life.

"Ma," I said from the living room, yelling into the kitchen, "I'm gonna go back earlier than I'd planned from Christmas break."

"You're going back to school early, Bobby?" she asked, puzzled. "My cooking not good enough for you anymore?"

"No, Ma. It's not your cooking. You're the one-and-only Greta the Great when it comes to cooking. You know that, Ma," I joked.

"You don't like your Christmas presents?" she said with a New York snap in her voice.

"No, no, no, Ma. Would you let me finish what I'm trying to say? I'm flying down to Houston to meet Ava's parents—and then drive back to Tulsa with her."

This surprised my mother. She stood speechless for a few seconds, trying to comprehend what I had just told her. Before this, I don't think my mother or my father had given much thought to the fact that I actually liked Ava as much as I did—probably because she was from Texas. Well, mostly because she was from Texas. I had never thought I would think seriously about marrying someone from Texas, either. I wasn't opposed to it, but if you had asked me at any time before I met Ava if I thought I would marry someone from the Lone Star State, I would have laughed. Ava and I were from two different worlds. I knew how Texans joked about New Yorkers. And I also knew how New Yorkers joked about Texans. It cut both ways.

I was excited and scared about going to meet Ava's parents—excited to see Ava, but scared of what her family might think of me. Meeting a girlfriend's family is always nerve-racking. On the plane ride to Houston I kept thinking, Will her father like me? Will her mother think I'm good enough for her daughter? What if I come across as a schlem? If they don't like me, will I still be able to date their daughter? Will they make fun of my Brooklyn accent? Will my manners be good enough? Can I be myself around them like I am with her? Will they make me wear a cowboy hat? And boots? Yeeeha! The Brooklyn Cowboy! Will I actually see people "moseying along?"

As I walked toward the front door of Ava's house, a million thoughts were going through my head. All I wanted to do was make a good impression and not make her parents wonder what Ava saw in me.

"Momma, Daddy, this is *Bawby*," Ava said to her parents with a smile and a confident manner in her tone. The way she introduced me put me at ease. She was so proud and confident that I lost my fears right there.

"Mr. and Mrs. Dorsett, it's a pleasure to meet you, sir, ma'am," I said as I firmly shook both of their hands.

They were both very cordial, but I could tell by the look on their faces after Ava so confidently introduced me that they realized for the first time—just as my parents had—that Ava and I were serious about each other.

"Bobby, it's a pleasure to meet *you*," Mr. Dorsett said in his deep, Texas-accented voice.

"Randall and I have heard so much about you, Bobby," Mrs. Dorsett said in her charming Houston accent. I knew then where Ava got her sweetness and charm—from her mother Linda.

We made an unlikely match, Ava and me, but we both felt good about it. Mr. D. was an ex-football player and also a well-known high school football coach in the Houston area. He and his family had ventured into business together to open a concrete plant. Many of his family members worked there. Ava's mother was now at home with Ava's younger sister Randa and volunteered at her church with various women's organizations.

The time with her family went better than I could have anticipated. Mr. and Mrs. D. were wonderfully nice, and they didn't wear cowboy boots or hats. And since they were both former physical education teachers and coaches, we immediately shared a common bond.

That last semester at school I carried eighteen credit hours plus three teaching assistantships, which was a heavy load. On a typical day I got up at 6:00 a.m., went to class and taught at my assistantships until 1:30 or 2:00 in the afternoon, sometimes later, went to baseball practice at about 2:00 until 6:00 or 7:00 at night, had dinner at the athletic dorm, and studied until midnight or so before going to bed to look forward to another day just like that one. From the time I got up, it was run-run-run all day until I fell in the bed, exhausted, eighteen hours and several miles of walking later.

With a maximum load of course work, teaching, and winter workouts for baseball, I didn't have time for much else except trying to spend at least some time with Ava. She understood that I was overloaded. Her support during this time made our relationship all the more special.

"You look tired, Bobby. Let me rub your neck, okay?" were some of the best words that I could've heard from Ava on those evenings that we studied together. Almost as good were, "How's my baby, tonight. Tired?" And then she would kiss me on the forehead. She knew that I had been running all day and that I was under pressure to finish school on time and try and keep up with baseball and all.

It's amazing how, when I got into the routine of having eighteen- and nineteen-hour days, every minute was scheduled and there was little wasted time. I learned to focus and narrow my priorities down to what really mattered, a very different mindset than when I had come into school as a freshman fours years earlier. If you compare freshman conversations with those of seniors, there's a stark contrast. It's a shift from, "How's my hair looking?" to "On my résumé— do employers really care about how many activity clubs I've been involved with these past four years?" Seniors know that the party's over and the real world is coming, sometimes faster than they'd like it to.

Still in the role of a back-up outfielder, I could now see more clearly than ever that my baseball career was not going to extend into the major leagues. I had another year of eligibility, but I knew my playing time wouldn't increase with all the top-notch current players and also the blue-chip prospects coming in that fall. I didn't pursue my extra year of eligibility. I accepted the fact that I hadn't yet reached my potential in baseball and maybe would not by the time I graduated.

In some ways, I'll have to admit, baseball had taken a backseat to another, more powerful love in my life. It was difficult to accept at first, but Ava helped to make it easier. After all, she was the more powerful love in my life.

"Ava, I think I'm finished with baseball," I told her, with

regret in my heart and a lump in my throat. I was finally admitting that I was good, but maybe not on the level to play pro ball. This was a hard thing for me to admit to myself, especially after seeing Uncle Rico become a star in the majors.

"You have another year of eligibility. Why don't you think about it?" she said. "You've always dreamed of playing in the majors. You could play minor league ball for a few years and after a while you'd be up in the majors before you knew it."

I sat quietly for about ten seconds and then glanced at her briefly. I then spoke straight down to the floor. "What if I wasn't meant to play professionally? What if I were supposed to play college ball and that's it? Maybe that's something I'll have to accept. I dunno, what do you think?"

She looked at me for a few moments, then walked over to me and put her arms around me, kissed me on the lips, and said, "Bobby, God gave you talent in baseball. He also gave you talent in coaching and many other areas of your life. Who's to say that you won't play baseball again? If we 'Seek first the kingdom of God, and His righteousness, then all these things will be added unto you.' And that includes baseball. So if your baseball career is over, then you've given God the best games of your life. That's all He asks—that we give our best to Him, so that He can give His best to us."

She was special. She had an insight and a strength that sometimes made me want to cry. She knew what to say and when to say it. To me it's a gift. A divine gift from God. She was my gift from Him. And an awesome one at that.

With thoughts of pro ball behind me, I now planned on moving to Texas after graduation to be near Ava. I had already contacted schools in the Friendswood area about doing my student teaching, which was all I had left to do to complete my teaching requirements. My degree was a bachelor's of science in health and physical education. I loved young people and recognized that I enjoyed coaching more and more because of the impact I could have on their lives in a positive, rewarding way. Shaping young people's lives through education and sports was to become essential to me. It was fulfilling in every sense of the word and also was one of my heart's deepest desires.

After I took my last and final exam at ORU, I went back to the dorm and sat quietly by myself, stunned. It seemed just yesterday that I had been a peanut-head freshman, registering for my first class, getting lost, feeling homesick for Sheepshead Bay, and then... BAM! My parents were coming down from New York in a few days to watch me graduate. *Where did the time go? Was I really here for four years? Was this a dream?* I looked at my closet and saw my cap and gown. That was all I needed to see.

I didn't have much time to reflect on what I'd done during my time in Tulsa. It was a blur. I had too many other things to try and wrap up between then and the graduation ceremony. My family was coming to Tulsa. Ava's family was coming to Tulsa. The Petrocellis meeting the Dorsetts. The Dorsetts meeting the Petrocellis. New York meeting Texas. I had no idea what was going to happen. What would my parents think? What would Ava's parents think? Would my father wear a cowboy hat? There's no way Greta would put on boots. Attilio, the urban cowboy? Greta the cowgirl? I don't think so. Not in this lifetime. But I know a lot of people who would pay good money to see that.

It was a stressful time for me. So much was happening at once with trying to close out the school year—I was finishing assistantships and moving all my stuff and saying goodbye to all my friends with whom I had lived for four years. And on top of that, my parents and Ava's parents were going to meet for the first time. Ava had every confidence in the world that it would be fine, and she was right. Mr. D. wasn't able to come because of work, but my parents met Mrs. D., Randa, and Ava's grandmother, Meemaw.

"Mom. Dad. I'd like you to meet Ava's mother, Linda Dorsett. And this is Ava's sister Randa." It was a little awkward, nonetheless. Mr. D. wasn't there, for one. Also, my parents are Brooklyn to a T, and they were still not completely convinced that I knew what I was doing in the love and dating department. And then, even though they were all adults, I knew they too were feeling some uneasiness and anxiety. We as young people need to give adults more credit. All four of them knew that what Ava and I had was real. For keeps.

I was so happy when that day was over.

Sadly, I wasn't able to properly say goodbye to my friends

and teachers. Maybe you never do. Maybe because you can't. After four of the most difficult yet exhilarating years of our lives together, there's no way to fully express in one minute the depths of our feelings while shaking hands and introducing them to family, then moving on to the next person you must say goodbye to.

"Congratulations, Bobby!" Rob said as he shook my hand, wearing his cap and gown just as I was.

"Thanks. Mom and Dad, this is Rob Knitt, a good buddy of mine from Wisconsin. We were on Youngblood together."

A few seconds later, "Petro, congratulations, man. Hey, I want you to meet my parents. They're here from Montana... "

"Joe, I'll talk to you later, buddy," I said as he walked away. But you never get to talk to them later. There is no later. Later turns into never. That's how it goes. That's the reality of it. We're here one day. Gone the next.

After graduation, I moved to Texas. Ava and I both felt strongly that we were going to be husband and wife sometime in the near future. School was over. That chapter in my life was now history. A new and exciting chapter, with Ava and my teaching and coaching career, was about to begin. I couldn't have been happier.

CHAPTER 4

FULL OF DREAMS

If I had thought Tulsa was hot, then Texas was Saudi Arabia hot. Fresh out of college, I went to work as a "yard boy" at the Dorsett Brothers Concrete Plant in Pasadena, Texas. That summer and fall of 1982 I cleaned and swept the offices, hosed down the trucks and floors, and greased the machinery, valves, fittings, and conveyor belt that carried the ingredients to make the concrete.

It was a dirty, grimy job and I hated it. It was humbling to be doing such difficult manual labor after just finishing my college degree. Most of the people in the plant were not, let's say, "sympathetic" toward New Yorkers, and I had to constantly put up with their comments and derogatory jokes about people from New York. This made it tough to look forward to work every day but, on the other hand, I had a job, for which I was grateful. Even though I was a college graduate, I came from a hard-working, blue-collar background. I would work at the concrete plant for six months, and then not ever do manual labor like that again unless I had to.

By the spring of 1983 I was student teaching in nearby Friendswood at the elementary, junior high, and senior high schools. In addition to teaching, I volunteered as a coach, assisting the varsity coach in off-season football and baseball. We did light workouts consisting of running, weight training, and stretching. This was such a positive and welcome change for me. I was doing something that I loved to do—coaching kids.

Pearland, where I lived, and Friendswood are suburban areas just south of Houston and not far from the beaches of Galveston. Not a bad place to settle down and raise a family, I thought as I became familiar with the area. Beautiful homes, plenty of land and open space, spread out, and a comfortable environment. It reminded me of some places in Tulsa. It had a similar feel.

Ava was finishing her psychology degree at the University of Houston–Clear Lake while working at the concrete plant, keeping books and doing clerical work. Somehow she still found time to volunteer at a women's shelter called "The Bridge." She absolutely loved it. Ava was a people person—very compassionate and sincere in counseling women who had come from broken and abusive marriages; and also working with unwed but pregnant girls, alcoholics, and drug addicts.

Ava lived at home with her parents. They had a beautiful place in Friendswood with a pool, jacuzzi, gorgeously kept gardens, and a nice piece of land. I liked going there after work because, to me, it was like going to a spa, a relaxing, luxurious spa.

The best friendships are those in which there is a balance in giving and taking. Problems can easily arise when one person is giving too much, and the other person is taking too much. Ava and I had a good balance of give and take. Ava always tried to show me with her actions that she cared for me. This made her that much more attractive, knowing that she was putting me before herself. I reciprocated. That's what love does—it reciprocates. It reflects good things back to the person who sends good things. It makes you care that much more—knowing that someone really cares, and wants the best for *you.*

On October 1, 1982, I took Ava out to a posh, classy restaurant. Our waiter started us with jumbo shrimp cocktails and garden fresh salad *du jour.* I guess they served different specialty salads every day. Next came the house soup that was absolutely out of this world, then lemon to refresh our palates, and we couldn't wait for the main course. I ordered filet mignon and she had lobster tail *a la supremeta.* I had absolutely no idea what a *la supremeta* was, but I was happy that Ava ordered it so I could finish what she couldn't. I could have steak *and* seafood. It was going to be a good night.

After more lemon to clean and refresh our palates and a dessert of cheesecake raspberria and chocolate mousse, Ava and I took a stroll in the gardens behind the restaurant. We strolled by a gazebo surrounded by exotic and seldom-seen flowers, and alongside a stream flowing gently through the garden. We sat outside in the cool breeze and talked about the evening and how much we had enjoyed the meal and spending a night out together.

It was dusk by now and the sun was just beginning to set. I stepped away from the wooden bench that we were sitting on, got down on one knee, and held her hand in mine.

"Ava Dorsett, do you think you wouldn't mind marrying me very much?" It was a line I had stolen from the original *Rocky* movie, in which Rocky asks Adrienne to marry him with the same quirky words. "What are you doing for the next, ahhh, fifty years or so," he says. "Do you think you wouldn't mind marrying me very much?"

After I said these words, Ava looked deep into my eyes and I could see the tears starting to form.

"Yes, Bobby Petrocelli," she said. "I would love to marry you."

My proposal came exactly one year after I had taken Ava out for our very first date. We planned a spring wedding to coincide with spring break at ORU so our friends there could come. The date was set for March. Anybody who's ever had to plan a wedding will tell you that it's a tremendous amount of work. They also say to start early because there are always details that you may forget. You learn a lot about your future mate in planning the event.

I'm a very detail-oriented person, and so was Ava. We complemented each other well and had all the bases covered: guest list, flowers, the wedding program, a photographer, the reception, honeymoon plans. Everything.

We were married in Friendswood United Methodist Church on March 12, 1983, with seven groomsmen, seven bridesmaids, and about three hundred in attendance. It was a wonderful wedding, a real celebration. Our families were there, our friends and loved ones. The reception was at the Dorsetts' home. This was truly an awesome day, and I was on cloud nineteen.

I hadn't slept very well the night before because I had all of my groomsmen plus my best man sleeping in my apartment together: Jay, Jakey, Riv, Craig Olson, Cheeks, and Bruno. I was glad they didn't have some crazy bachelor's party for me the night before. I was so exhausted I wouldn't have enjoyed it. Instead, after the rehearsal dinner, we had gone back to my apartment and hung out and talked until the wee hours of the morning. That was just what I wanted to do. These were my best friends, like brothers to me. I just wanted to spend time with them and laugh at some of the crazy and stupid things we had done together over the years.

I was nervous that day because I wanted everything to go well and everyone to have a good time. So much planning had gone into this wedding, I wanted it to be the best we could possibly have. I arrived at the church an hour and fifteen minutes early so that we all could get dressed and relax before the ceremony. As we got dressed in the back choir room of the church, my brother-in-law Nicky couldn't find his bow tie anywhere and started to get panicky. He and Ava's cousin Bill were the only two groomsmen who hadn't stayed with the rest of us in my apartment the night before.

"I'm gonna get your sista," said Nicky in a testy and impatient voice. "I'm gonna get Debbie. She forgot to give me my bow tie. I can't go out there without a bow tie. It looks stupid!" Nicky had already torn up the room looking for the tie, but without any luck. Finally, fifteen minutes before the ceremony, he found it hanging on a hanger with the rest of his tuxedo stuff.

When all this was going on, it started to settle in on me what a big plunge this was—to be getting married. I tried not to be hyper, but I didn't do a good job of being calm. I kept moving and pacing, moving and pacing, moving and pacing. I was so happy when the time came, and I could leave that choir room and start walking toward the sanctuary. Down the corridor I walked. In the distance I heard the buzz of excitement coming from the sanctuary. This was it. There was no turning back. Closer, closer, closer we walked. I took a deep breath right outside the side entrance to the front of the sanctuary and prayed a silent prayer, "God, thank you for today, a day I've waited all of my life for. Amen." Then I walked to the front of the sanctuary with Bruno, my best man.

I'll never forget the moment I saw Ava appear in the door wearing her wedding gown. She was stunning. Absolutely stunning. I had such a rush of emotion upon seeing her and knowing that she was about to become my wife that I almost cried right there. If I hadn't been completely exhausted from the planning and events leading up to the wedding itself, I would've cried my eyes out. But I didn't. And I'm glad I held back.

She slowly walked toward me and I could see her "Ava smile," the one where her top lip got thin, she showed her perfect white teeth, and her dimples deepened in her cheeks. I couldn't take my eyes off her. She hypnotized me with her radiance and the sheer joy that beamed from her infectious smile.

"Who gives this woman to this man?" the pastor asked.

"Her mother and I," Mr. D. said.

I took Ava's hand. Goose-bumps covered me at the mere touch of her skin, and it reminded me of the very first time I had kissed her in Keystone State Park in Oklahoma. In a few moments I would kiss her again. This time it would be different. This time it would be as Mrs. Robert James Petrocelli.

I couldn't wait for her lips to touch mine. It would be the best kiss since the first, and the sweetest of my life.

That night we stayed in Houston and flew to Acapulco, Mexico, the next morning for what would be an incredible honeymoon. The sun was shining brightly, the sand was white as snow, and the water was crystal clear. I could see all the fish and coral in the Gulf.

"Ava, should we move here?" I joked.

"I've already got the house picked out," she jabbed back at me. "See that grass hut over there?" I laughed, and then she kissed me. "You think I'm kidding, don't you?"

It was a different world. This was paradise. If this were any indication of how our life together would be, then why hadn't we got married sooner? I could live with this. Give me that grass hut over there. No problem at all. We laid on the sun-drenched beach late in the afternoon after a full day of parasailing and shopping. My baby was right beside me, and she looked both delicious and inviting. As I laid there I peered at Ava through my sunglasses, squinting and smiling at her.

"Bobby, what are you thinking about?" she asked.

"My wife," I said as I gazed at her. It felt good to say

those words. *Mrs. Petrocelli,* I thought to myself. *Mrs. Ava Petrocelli. Mrs. Ava Robert Petrocelli. Mrs. Ava Robert James Petrocelli.* This is the one I had been looking for. Mrs. A.R.J.P. It had a ring to it. That was *my* girl. She was mine. She belonged solely to me. And nobody else on this beach could have her. This was one of those moments, a time you can say to yourself, "This is good. This is very good."

I had my youth. I had my love. And I had a bright career ahead as a teacher and coach.

When I finished student teaching at Friendswood High School, I accepted a full-time position as a health education teacher and coach at Santa Fe High in nearby Alta Loma. It was a great situation. I coached football and baseball. My typical day started 7:00 each morning and ended between 7:00 and 11:00 p.m., after all the kids had gone home following practice for whichever sport I was coaching at the time.

I loved to coach, but more than that I loved the kids. They hung on my every word as if it were the most important thing in the world. For some reason coaches are looked upon with higher esteem than other teachers and, in many cases, respected more than parents. It's part of the job. It comes with the territory. It's how our society looks at members of the coaching profession—as mentors, as role models.

"Now listen to me carefully," I would rally them before a game. "I want every one of you to give me everything you've got out on that field today. This team has been mouthing off and talking trash all week long that they're gonna kick our butts. It's true—they have better athletes than we do. It's true—they are bigger and stronger than we are. It's also true—they are undefeated up to this point midway through the season.

"But let me tell you something right here and now. If you go out there and play four quarters of hard football like you've been practicing all week, you're not only going to win this game, you're going to stomp this team. And when it's over, I don't want anybody to brag. Because winners don't brag. Men don't brag. Winners—and men—shake the other team's hand and say, 'Good game. I enjoyed it.' And when this season's over and you're long gone from Santa Fe High School in Alta Loma, Texas, I want each of you to know this: nobody remembers the score, nobody remembers who wins and who loses. It's your attitude that's never forgotten."

Ava and I served as youth leaders at Lakewood Church. Amongst our other duties, we volunteered to help with the Sunday morning program, which included several hundred kids ranging in age from thirteen to eighteen. This ministry was important to us because we both recognized the values that had been instilled into our lives as youngsters growing up in a Christian environment. The group of kids was so large that often we held a separate service just for the teens.

Ava's grandmother, Meemaw, had a beach house at Bolivar Island, and it was a great getaway. Other times we drove to her house in Kingwood and visited her for a Saturday night and stayed until Sunday. She loved to cook and we loved to eat her cooking. How's that for complementing each other? Meemaw always made me feel welcome and at home.

"Bobby, how are things with your job?" she'd ask, really wanting to know.

That's the thing I appreciated about her. She really wanted to know the answers to the questions she asked. She wasn't just asking to ask. She was genuine and I got the same sense of humble Christ-like love from Meemaw that I had received from Pastor Greco in New York. Ava and I both looked forward to the times we spent with Meemaw. Visiting her was a nice change of pace from the routine of our everyday lives. Being with Meemaw gave us a different perspective on life, one that I missed with my own grandparents in New York. I think they all would've gotten along together—Nanny, Meemaw, and Beepa. They had great nicknames, at least.

From March to August 1983, Ava and I lived in a small apartment with limited amenities. I didn't like feeling cooped up, and couldn't wait for the right time to move into a bigger place. We really wanted a house, but couldn't afford one. Brand new, more luxurious apartments with cable television and a swimming pool were being completed right across the street from us. It was a glorious August day when we moved over to "The Heights."

This was better. It was much cleaner and brighter. Ava and I danced on our carpet in the new apartment. "Burning. Burning. Disco Inferno. Burning. Burning." I can still hear that music playing. The movie *Saturday Night Fever* was based on my neighborhood in Brooklyn, but Travolta had nothing on me that night. I could've taught him plenty of dance moves. We were finally in a bigger place. *Yesssssss!* Goodbye little matchbox. Hello shoe box.

I love the intimacy of marriage. I love the holding, the hugging, the snuggling, the "spooning," the warmth, and the simplicity of knowing that my wife is there for me. That's what I like. The knowing. It's a peaceful feeling. A strength and security. That wonderful sense of oneness. Two halves making one whole, like pieces to a puzzle fitting together so well—by design. I really felt that with Ava. She saw me when my hair stuck straight up in the air like Don King's. She saw me when I woke up in the morning and my eyes looked like Mr. Magoo's. And she smelled me when I got home from a full day of football practice in the hot sun and I hummed so badly that the neighborhood pets all ran from me when they saw me coming. She knew me at my best, she knew me at my worst, and you know something— she loved me just the same. That's love. That's friendship. That's intimacy. That's marriage.

After two and a half years of apartment living, Ava and I were more than anxious to move into a house. But, with interest rates as high as they were in 1985, we couldn't afford to buy a home just then. Instead, we found a four-bedroom house that we could rent in a brand new housing development in League City. 501 Landing Blvd. was our first home. We moved into our house on Labor Day weekend, and we were really excited about it.

"Baby, I can't believe it. We're really in a house. *Ahhhhhhhhhh!*" she screamed with excitement. "See that. I can even scream and no one upstairs or downstairs will start banging on the walls and yell, 'Hey, shut up down there. Don't you people ever sleep?'

"And you can laugh as loud as you want. You can watch your 'Three Stooges' and 'Honeymooners' tapes at any time of the day or night and laugh your heart out, and no one will think that you're a demented hyena or something—well, you are that, but at least no one else will think so, honey," she said. A mischievous smile crossed her face.

"Come on," I said, "let's look at the bedrooms. There's four: One for you and three for me. See how generous I am?"

We ran from room to room like kids playing, and I tackled her along the way in each room.

"Ava's trying for the second bedroom. She's got a slight opening, but—*noooo!* She's dragged down at the five-yard line. Oh, what a game-saving tackle by Bobby Pet Butkus of the Bears!"

"No! *Drrrrrrrrrr*. There's a flag on the play," Ava shot back. "Illegal use of the hands."

"What are you talking about? That's *legal*. You're my wife!" I exclaimed, and I tickled her in all the right places: her stomach, her ribs, and her knees.

"*Stop, Bobby. Stop, Bobby. Stop, Bobby. Stop...* " she laughed as I went to work on her mercilessly.

It was a beautiful house. As well as four bedrooms, it had two baths, a living room with a fireplace, a beautiful bay window in the master bedroom, an alarm system, sprinklers, ceiling fans, a wooden deck, and a microwave.

I could describe our new house with one word—space. That's what we liked. Space. And we had plenty of it, inside and out. I put my drums in one of the extra bedrooms so I could bang away to my heart's content. I'd bang, bang, bang away. You see, I had to make up for all the lost time I couldn't play living in the cramped apartments. It was a good way to relieve stress. At least for me it was.

Outside we had a big yard, and because it was a new development, we were the very first house you saw when you came into the neighborhood. A large, grassy area more than a quarter-mile long separated our house from the street coming into the complex. We liked the privacy of having no one on the entire right side of us, nothing except this grass field. In fact, it was so big that I practiced chipping golf balls out there. It was kind of like having my own private mini-course. I should have called it Petro's Greens. "Arnold Petro Palmer steps up to the plate. Oh, there's a blooper to left field, it's gonna drop in for a base hit. One run will score and they're waving in the runner from second base. What a soft touch from Petro Palmer. He's going to hit for the cycle today." As a kid, I always dreamed of having my own baseball field—a big, wide open, green baseball field. This was close enough. This was my "field of dreams."

The house was solid brick, which we really liked. Solid, heavy-duty brick. Occasionally, bad storms and tornadoes posed a threat in any part of Texas, so the brick made us feel safer than if it were wood. Ava and I talked about waiting for a brick home once we were finally able to afford a house because there's something psychologically satisfying about having brick, too. At least to us there was. More of a fortress kind of feel to me. This is my domain. My castle. Nothing can harm us inside these stone walls. We were young, strong, and still invincible.

A house is not a home until it has a woman's special touch. I'd been to many of my buddies' homes who lived by themselves or with other guys. It's not the same as when a woman adds her touch. Ava loved to decorate. She collected porcelain dolls and decorative pillows that she placed on the ledge of the bay window in our bedroom. Each one had a story behind it. She should have written them down— she may have been the next Dr. Seuss. The dolls and pillows would be keepsakes that we'd pass on to our children, our grandchildren, and our great grandchildren. We had it all planned out. There was a lifetime ahead of us. Ava was twenty-three. I was twenty-four. We talked about little bambinos in the near future. A bambinette for her. A bambino for me. We were simple people. We just didn't want twins to start off with. Maybe later, but not then.

Our bed was right up against the bay window in the master bedroom. We loved seeing the stars at night flickering in the sky before we fell asleep in each other's arms. Talk about a romantic atmosphere—it was wonderful. Sometimes I would lie there at night with my baby and just gaze at the stars. We joked that there were "stars in our eyes." There were. I would sing, "Hey there. You with the stars in your eyes... " Ava's eyes would glisten in the moonlight. The way the light fell gently onto her face through the bay window sent tingles through me. Sometimes I'd wake up in the middle of a clear starry night and just watch her sleep. Have you ever done that? Watched your spouse sleep?

"Bobby, what are you doing? Are you staring at me again? What is this, some secret fetish of yours, watching me sleep?" she would playfully ask.

"No, baby. I just can't believe how beautiful you look when you sleep,"

"Get real. Beautiful? You wouldn't say that if the lights weren't off and you could see that I'm not wearing any makeup."

Sleep-watching. It's what newlyweds do. Part of the romance, I guess. And it never wore off for us. Maybe because I loved her so much. Maybe because I knew she'd do anything for me. When someone is that committed and dedicated to you, you get a strong feeling inside, a longing that makes you think about that person every minute of the day. You may be in the middle of your workday and suddenly that longing will tug at your heart. Only my love can fill that space because she knows me like a book. When I act like "The Coach." When I act like a kid. When I let my guard down. When I'm the Bobby no one else has seen. She's my safe haven to run to. A shelter from the storms of life. A refuge in times of discouragement.

Full moons were the best. The light was so bright you could literally see shadows. Shadows and silhouettes. They led to more playful evenings. Understated, soft blue moonbeams danced throughout our bedroom on those nights. There seemed to be a warmth in its rays. Warm moonbeams.

"Ava, look at this," I said one night with the enthusiasm of an eight year old. I was making shadow animals with my hands as the moon shone through our bedroom window. "Here's a rabbit. How about this one?" I asked as I made a crocodile.

"That's easy, honey. You've got to do better ones," she softly said, half asleep.

"Uh, oh. Here's a roadrunner," I warned as I ran my fingers like a running bird over her back. "The roadrunner's looking for the coyote. Is he here?" I asked, moving my hand to the back of her neck.

"*Yelp!*" she screamed, "Bobby, don't start *tickling meeeeee...* " It was too late. The game had already begun.

For the first three weeks in our new home my father stayed with us. He was visiting from New York and, because he had had a stroke, he got around using a wheelchair. I remember him being so proud of my house. He bragged about how beautiful it was. I was glad that he shared this time with us because it was he who had drilled into me the importance of family and of working hard to provide for them. My father is quite a guy. Three weeks with Dad was about the right amount, though. He kept us going. And going. And going. What can I say? He's Attilio! They broke the mold when they made him.

Dad flew back to Brooklyn, and we got back to just Ava and me. It had been nice to have company, but it was nice to have the house to ourselves again. Quiet. Peaceful. Just the two of us.

CHAPTER 5

THAT DAY

I got home about seven o'clock that Wednesday night, October 23, and collapsed in front of the television to wind down from the day. The Kansas City Royals were playing the St. Louis Cardinals in the World Series.

Wednesday was really the only day Ava and I would spend quality time together that week. On Mondays I had class at the University of Houston–Clear Lake where I was working on my master's degree in counseling education. Ava spent Tuesday evening at The Bridge, the women's shelter at which she volunteered. Thursday and Friday were dedicated to football during the season.

Here it was the end of October and they were still playing baseball. Gets later and later every year. I had taken the T.V. outside to the deck because it was a gorgeous evening. I was watching Tom Nieto, a catcher for the Cardinals who had played baseball with me at ORU. It was cool, quiet, and uneventful. Ava came out and watched a little of the game with me. She knew I loved sports, especially this time of year during the World Series.

"Who's winning?" she asked.

"Oh, for cryin' out loud!" I yelled at the T.V. set. "Now you loaded up the bases. This guy couldn't find the plate with a softball!"

Ava giggled at me because I always talked to the T.V. when I got mad about how the game was going.

"You want more ice tea?" she asked softly, sliding into my lap.

"I'll get some at the end of the... "

I never finished the sentence. She kissed me with one of her warm, soft kisses and, for an instant, I forgot where I was and that I was watching the game—that's how good it was. She smiled her cute smile, the one where her mouth curled up on the side and I could see her dimples really

well. It was Ava's "I did it to you again!" smile. She loved to
kiss me mid-sentence so that I couldn't get the words out. It
was one of those little games she played, and you know
what? I didn't mind one bit. Not one little bit.

I don't remember much about the game after that. I
finally turned the T.V. off because the light from the set
and the announcer's voice were distracting me from the
business at hand—you know what I mean. What can I say?
Some things are more important than baseball. That's why
they made VCRs.

On Thursdays during football season, Ava got up at 6:00
a.m., showered and got ready for work. She then went into
the kitchen for breakfast. I waited until she was finished,
then took a shower and got ready myself. After I showered,
shaved, and did my hair, I went into the kitchen and sat
down to have a bowl of cereal, orange juice, and toast.

"We're almost out of milk, baby," I said, as Ava returned
to the bathroom to finish getting ready and touch up.

"I'll pick some up after work, okay?"

"Skim milk, all right, honey?"

"Skim milk, Bobby," she said as if she'd heard it a hundred times. Actually, she had. I finished eating, went back
into the bathroom, and brushed my teeth. This was really
the only time that we shared the bathroom together.

"I have to go to Wharton today," I said, "so I won't be
home until 10:30 or so. Remember, today is Nicholas' birthday. If you have time, can you call Debbie and wish him a
'Happy Birthday' from us?"

"I'll do it when I get home tonight."

"I don't want him to think we forgot about it."

"I'll do it tonight," she assured me as she kissed me on
the neck.

I got dressed in my street clothes that day: a shirt, a tie,
and pair of slacks. I didn't need to wear coaching attire
because on Thursday mornings I could go in a little bit
later—for a short team meeting—instead of a morning practice. That afternoon, our freshmen team would travel to
play an away game.

Ava and I both left the house around 7:00. We both had
to be at work by 7:30. She went her direction, to her job at
the concrete plant. And I went mine.

This particular Thursday was busier than usual. It was so hectic that I didn't get a chance to call Ava, to at least touch base with her as I normally did during the day. Several times I thought I had a minute to call, but every time I started to, somebody yelled for me to do something. I left with the freshmen team for their game in Wharton, eighty miles away, and was on the road for a couple hours. When I got there I decided not to make a long distance call. I knew Ava would go straight from work to the women's shelter as she always did.

"Get him, get him, *get him!*" I yelled at our defensive line during the thick of the game. I watched as five of our boys converged on their quarterback and sacked him for an eleven-yard loss. "Atta boy, Kevin! That's how you pursue! Let 'em know who you are! You're the boss! Atta baby!" I yelled.

The rest of our players on the sideline roared as the defense again stifled Wharton's high-powered offense. The teams lined up for the next play from scrimmage. "Don't jump! Don't jump! He's trying to pull you off-sides!" I exclaimed as their quarterback barked, "*Hut* one. *Hut* two. *Hut*, hut… *hut!*" Nobody went for it. "*Hut*," he barked again, and the center snapped the ball. Our defensive line sliced through their line like a knife through butter and again gang tackled the QB.

Again, a huge roar came from our guys on the sideline. The momentum was ours and we couldn't be stopped. It's a great feeling when that happens for your team—but a sick feeling when you're on the other end. I've been on both sides of momentum swings, so I know what it feels like. Our boys played inspired ball that day. I was proud. Really proud. We beat a good team that day. A talented and well-coached team.

When the game was over, we hung around to cheer on the junior varsity team. Gary Causey, our assistant principal at Santa Fe, joined me on the sidelines and we chatted about the game and which boys were playing well and which boys were not. We eventually began to talk about life—and then about God.

"Petro, if God is so good, why do people have problems? Why does God allow people to suffer?" he asked.

I paused for a second as I thought about my answer. He

had asked a good question, one that I had to ponder for a moment.

"Well," I finally answered, "sometimes problems occur because people make foolish and stupid choices. We can't blame God for that. It's not his fault. If he didn't give us a free will and the chance to make our own choices, we'd be nothing more than robots, following whatever was programmed into our computers and memory banks."

We talked more about free will and making correct choices. It was a good talk because Gary was interested in what I believed and had to say.

We boarded the buses to return to Sante Fe and arrived back at the high school around 10:00 p.m. I hung around until all the kids were picked up and gone. Some nights I'd drive kids home but, fortunately, I didn't have to that night. I got away at 10:30, knowing I had to be back early the next morning for another team meeting, and to take care of any football business that hadn't been finished that night. The next night, Friday, would be busy, too. I was scouting Friendswood.

I had been going since 6:00 a.m. and was tired as I pulled into my neighborhood. There wasn't a more welcome sight in all the world than our red brick home across my grassy field, Petro's Greens. What a great feeling to be home! I pulled into the driveway, opened up the garage door, parked the car, and walked into the kitchen where Ava greeted me as she normally did, with a hug and a kiss.

"Are you tired, baby?" she asked as I slumped down into my dining room chair.

"Yep," I said, "but we won today. The boys really played well. Really well! I was proud of them because they played like they wanted to win. That was the key. They wanted to win—instead of trying not to lose."

There was a sparkle in her eye that night as she kissed me a second time. She knew how to give me that look to let me know that I was home but, more importantly, that I was hers. I was safe. Free to be myself—whichever mood I was in. At school I was the teacher, I was the coach, and also the encourager. But now, at the end of the day, I was the tired little boy. Imagine that. Here I am, six foot two and two hundred pounds, and this little woman gives me a smile that makes me want to cry inside. That's what love does. It breaks you down, chews you up, and spits you out. It makes you human. Anyone who's ever been in love will tell you that it's one of the best feelings in the world—that feeling of oneness, that bonding, that surrender, that comfortable sense of vulnerability.

Men won't admit it, but women make us feel this way. Who really has the power? Who really is the boss? Any man will tell you, it's not us.

Ava was always upbeat and energetic on these late nights. It was a great feeling to come home to a wife who was as happy to see me as I was to see her. We knew we wouldn't be able to spend time together until later on that weekend, on Saturday, perhaps. Friday nights were for scouting. Ava knew the routine—this was my third season coaching football. On Saturday mornings I'd go back to school and break down game films, so I'd only get to see Ava at about two or three o'clock on Saturday afternoons during the season. It was a long week, and I had to repeat this cycle until November, when the season finally ended. So I cherished every moment I was able to spend with Ava during football season. She understood that it was part of my job. She was good that way—she knew what I had to do. There is always sacrifice involved when in a profession like mine. Every coach's wife will tell you that.

I walked into the kitchen and there it was—a big bowl of rigatoni with sauce. It was nice and hot. Ava had great timing, like a sixth sense. They say that after couples have been together for awhile, they develop this inner clock that lets them know what the other is doing. I don't know if it's true, but I do know that Ava's timing was extremely good. And even though she wasn't *Italiano*, she made a mighty mean sauce. A Texas-Sicilian kind of meat sauce. The kind that put so much hair on your chest the barber has to use a lawn mower for a shave and a trim.

"Ava, I think that you have relatives in Palermo and Napoli that you're not telling me about. Your father told me his great grandfather changed his name from Dorsettini to Dorsett when he came to America!"

She laughed and swatted at my shoulder. "You're silly," she said, emphasizing her squeaky Texas drawl to let me know she had no Italian whatsoever in her genes—from any generation. She was pure Texas Belle.

Ava had eaten hours before, so she just sat and talked with me. I was just so happy to be home and to be with my baby that it didn't matter what we talked about. We usually talked about how one another's days had gone, things like that.

"So how were things at The Bridge today?"

"Oh, about the same today. No big flare-ups or arguments this time."

She always sat with me while I ate. Most of the time after getting home late like that, I'd eat and she wouldn't, but she always sat with me. Maybe some people wouldn't consider that a big deal, but I liked that she sat in her chair, with no food, just to be with me. It's a simple thing, I know, but it's an important thing. She conveyed a message to me while she sat and watched me eat: She was saying that she loved me. She didn't have to say the words. I knew it. Her actions spoke volumes about the way she felt.

It was eleven o'clock when I got up from the table. "More, Bobby?" Ava asked.

"No, thanks. I'm packed." She always asked me if I had had enough, and I always said, "I'm packed." I knew she would ask, and she knew how I would respond. It was like an inside joke. A game. A chemistry between us. That made it great.

Ava cleaned up the dishes and I went to take a shower. Showers felt good after days like this. I could rinse the weight of the day off me, and Ava wouldn't kick me out of bed for being all grungy and mealy. She didn't have to say the words. Her actions spoke volumes.

When I finished showering I came back out to the living room, where Ava was straightening up. I felt refreshed and relaxed.

"Did the tape record?" I asked her.

"Sure did," she said.

One of my favorite things to do on Thursday nights after the long football day was watch "The Honeymooners," which I recorded every week. I liked "The Honeymooners" as much as I liked "The Three Stooges." And that's a lot. I could sit for hours on end and watch those two shows. I'd laugh and laugh and laugh. It was the type of show that I could have one of those good, hearty, full-bodied, stomach-hurting laughs that we all need once in a while just to remain sane. I was more than ready for it.

Norton and Ralph were going to be on the "Beat the Clock" show in this episode. They were practicing stunts in Ralph's apartment, rolling eggs down a long trough, catching each one, and putting them in the basket before the eggs broke. Ralph rolled them down and Norton tried to catch them and bring them back up to Ralph.

It was a funny show, all right, but my attention was diverted from the television when Ava sat in my lap.

"I heard they taped these shows in front of a live audience," Ava said.

"Yep. If you watch real closely, you can see them mess up sometimes. The chemistry on this show is phenomenal. They knew each other so well—like they knew what the other person was going to do."

"That's why it's so good," Ava said. She was right. The classic television shows are the ones with casts who worked well together.

"We have chemistry, Bobby," Ava softly whispered in my ear as she nibbled on my lobe. "We have anatomy and physiology, too, don't we, honey?"

I somehow forgot about Ralph, Norton, and Alice on the television. I could watch that tape anytime. I was with my own "honeymooner." We cuddled together in the recliner chair, talking more about how her day had gone, and how hectic the day had been for both of us.

"Do you think some year you'll stop coaching football, Bobby?" she playfully but earnestly asked me. I knew what she was getting at. It was times like these that I wished I could have collected all those hundreds—no thousands—of hours and cashed them in for more moments like this.

We talked about other things while cuddled together in the recliner. "Did you have a chance to call Debbie and wish Nicholas a Happy Birthday?" I asked with anticipation.

"No... I didn't. I was so busy with everything—one thing after another—that I didn't get a chance to. I'm sorry, Bobby."

It was past eleven and New York is an hour ahead of Texas. I didn't want to call and wake him up. "We can call him in the morning to see if he's gotten the card we sent." I told her.

We talked about my family flying down from Brooklyn to be with us for Thanksgiving. They were all coming: My mom, dad, Debbie and her husband Nicky, Nicholas, and my younger sister Chrissy. My dad had already purchased the plane tickets, and I was looking forward to the visit.

"Do you think they'll like it?" Ava asked, referring to the house.

"If they don't, they can sleep in the yard," I joked back at her. "Of course they'll like it, baby," I reassured her. "You've done a wonderful job with the house, Ava-la."

Ava mentioned that, since it was the end of October, she'd like to go Christmas shopping that weekend. "We could go on Saturday after you're done watching game films," she said.

"Where do you wanna go? Baybrook or the Galleria?" I asked, referring to popular malls nearby.

"Can we do both?" she asked with a child-like smile of anticipation on her face.

"Whatever you wanna do, baby, that's what we'll do."

She smiled and squinted her eyes with approval that the plan was set. It was the type of moment that I loved, because I knew she would look forward to it like a kid anticipating a trip to the candy store. Just knowing that she was excited and happy made me happy as well. We connected at that moment. There's something deeply satisfying in a relationship, when you get those rare and sometimes too few and far-between moments of connection and bonding. But when it happens—it makes everything worthwhile.

When we finished talking, Ava got up, went to the bathroom to freshen up, and got ready for bed. It was about 11:30. "The Honeymooners" was over. She peeked her head around the corner. "Good night," she said, meaning she was headed for bed and I could stay up if I wanted to.

"Good night," I said. I rewound the tape and turned off the T.V. and VCR. I went into the kitchen to perform my "before I go to bed" ritual. I checked the oven. It was off. The stove? Off. The microwave. Yep. Refrigerator? Closed. Everything locked up? Garage door. Check. Back door? Good. Front door? Double locked. That's it. Everything the way it should be. My security duties were over. I could now go to bed with peace of mind, knowing that I hadn't forgotten anything. The king had checked the castle, and the castle was secure. I turned off the lights behind me as I made my way to our bedroom, making one final stop in the bathroom to brush my teeth.

Ava was already snuggled comfortably in the bed. I cuddled up beside her because my side of the bed was still cold. That's another simple pleasure that's easily taken for granted—getting in a bed that has already been warmed for you.

We lay there together. "I think my family's gonna love the house, Ava, absolutely love it," I said. She reached over and squeezed my thigh—meaning "Thank you for saying that." I remembered what my dad had said, and how proud he was of me for having the house, and working hard to provide for Ava. I wrapped my arms around her and enveloped her completely as we lay in the "spoon" position.

She kissed me goodnight, then I lay there quietly for several minutes trying to relax and let my mind slow down. I was wound up from the day and my mind was still racing. I thought about the game: Kevin, who had played a great game on defense; Gary Causey, and what we had talked about—wondering if he was lying in bed with his wife, not being able to sleep because he was thinking about our conversation, too. A few minutes passed. The clock showed 11:35. I looked out the bay window and saw the flickering stars. It was a calm night, a calm night after a hectic day. I was glad the week was almost over. I started to think back about specific plays in our game that afternoon, things that had worked, things that had not. For some reason, I always second-guess the day's events at night when I'm lying quietly in bed. Maybe it's natural. For me it was. I liked this part of the day because it was a time to reflect, a time to unwind and let my mind rest after racing for the entire day.

Five more minutes passed and I still couldn't sleep. I looked out again at the stars. *It's a vast universe*, I thought. *All the stars and planets out there. Four billion people in the world and God loves each one of us. Yes, indeed. He had given me a good life. A good job. A new house. A loving wife. What more could I ask for?* I thought again about Ava as I looked up at the porcelain dolls and decorative pillows on the windowsill, and thought of all the stories behind each one of them. I had a good woman. I had been truly blessed.

The clock now showed 11:40. I got out of bed and stumbled through the dark to the kitchen to get a glass of milk. Milk helped me sleep. It settled me down. I would wake up with sour breath the next morning, but that's the breaks. I opened the refrigerator and found that the carton was empty, so I had a glass of water instead.

When I came back to bed I mentioned to Ava that there was no milk. Half asleep, she mumbled, "I'll get some first thing in the morning." I touched her on her side to say that I appreciated her doing that. I said a few prayers out loud for the two of us. I liked to do that before we went to sleep. This was important to me. Starting the day with prayer and ending the day with prayer. You have to do things right.

"God, thank you for today and for being with us during our trip to Wharton for the game. Thank you for keeping us from any injuries. I pray that you be with each of the kids and other coaches as they sleep tonight. Give them a deep, restful sleep. I pray that tomorrow will be a good day and we'll be able to accomplish all that you have for us to do. Be with our families tonight, and keep them safe. Thank you for being with Ava at her job and in her work at the women's shelter. I pray that you will continue to use her there, to bless the ladies and girls who are going through so much adversity and difficulty in their lives. Give us a restful and deep sleep this evening. We pray all these things in your name. Amen."

Ava mumbled, "Amen." I kissed her on the cheek and turned over to go to sleep. It was now between 11:40 and 11:45. It had been a good day. A full day. I had accomplished a lot that day, and had many things to be proud of, but now it was time to sleep. A time to relax. A time to let the cares of the day just drift into oblivion. I lay there quietly for a few moments with my eyes open. Finally, I closed my eyes and fell into a deep, peaceful sleep, the kind that you want every night of the week. A perfect ending to another full day.

CHAPTER 6

RUDE AWAKENING

Approximately one hour later I woke up, but instead of being in my bed, I was in the dining room. The dining room was next to the bedroom, and I was leaning up next to the dining-room window. As I tried to pick up my head for the first time and shake out the grogginess, bright lights shone in my eyes from the right. I didn't know where they came from. I looked to my left and saw a haze, a cloud of smoke. This seemed odd.

Lights flickered to the left through a big opening and a breeze blew in. I tried to focus my eyes and at the same time smelled something foul: sulfur, tar, burning rubber, and plastic. It was a horrible stench. A cold chill went through me, the kind that goes right to your bones. Again, I tried to focus my eyes and rub the crusty sleep out of them. I was definitely in the dining room, and the wall between my dining room and bedroom was missing. That didn't make sense. Where was the wall? I saw the lights again and realized a full-size pickup truck sat motionless in front of me. I was beside the front right tire. I shook my head, trying to shake the cobwebs out. *I must be dreaming. What's this truck doing in the middle of my dining room?* I thought. *What's going on here? Is that a blue and white pickup truck in the middle of my house?*

I stood up as best as I could. I was near the passenger door of the truck. The stench was stronger than ever, and a cloud of smoke surrounded me. Then I saw a man step out of the driver's side of the truck. He was a large man, scraggly, wearing a baseball cap. A gash sliced his forehead and something trickled down it. It was red but I couldn't completely focus to tell exactly what it was. I asked myself, *Who is this man in the middle of my dining room?*

He saw me. "Is there somebody else in the house?" he asked.

Is there somebody else in the house? I thought. *Who is this strange man in the middle of my house?* His question echoed faintly in the back of my mind as I tried desperately to process thoughts coherently. *Is there somebody else in the house? What's this truck doing in the middle of my dining room? Is there somebody else in the house? Who's this strange man standing here asking questions? Where is my bed? What am I doing in the dining room? Is there somebody else in the house? What's this stench? What's this smoke? What is going on here? Is there somebody else in the house? SOMEBODY ELSE IN THE HOUSE? AVA! My wife! Where is my wife?*

I freaked out and started running around the truck. I ran into my bathroom trying to turn on lights, thinking that if I could just get some light I could see more clearly what was going on. I flicked the switch in the bathroom but, for some reason, the lights didn't come on. That was odd. I ran out of the bathroom and back into my bedroom. I leaned up against the wall and searched for the switch. Finally, I found it, but it was no good. No lights. I ran into the kitchen. Nothing. The hallway. Nope. The living room. The foyer. Still none. I tried every single lamp. I even hit the switch for the T.V. No dice. I couldn't get anything to work. There was no power.

I stumbled to the far side of the house to a second bathroom. I reached around the wall, flicked the switch and—*bingo*—lights came on. Relieved, I stepped into the bathroom. Something had been dripping on my legs. It was on my arms, too, but I didn't know what it was. I felt something crunch in my mouth, so I spit into the sink. I lifted up my head and looked in the mirror. I was groggy and my eyes had to try to focus.

I stepped back in shock. I could barely see my face in the reflection in the mirror. There was a stream—a waterfall of red—flowing down my face. It was blood. I could now see it going down my chest and onto my arms, over my underwear, and my legs, and onto the floor. I felt that crunching in my mouth again. Again I spit. Huge hunks of bloody glass plopped into the sink. I searched for a towel and found a white one. I turned on the faucet and put the towel under the water to dampen it. I wiped my face, thinking that if I cleaned up the blood, I'd have a better idea of how badly I was hurt. The towel made a scrunching sound as it scraped over pieces of glass that were imbedded in my cheek.

With the blood temporarily gone, I saw a huge hole in my cheek and stuck my tongue through it. Again, I spit a large chunk of blood and glass out of my mouth into the bowl. The blood had started to flow again as I watched it splash into the sink. Wiping my face again, I threw the towel into the basin and turned to leave the bathroom. I slipped on blood on the way out.

I walked through the hallway, past the other bedrooms, and into the main opening to the living room, not knowing where Ava was. I stood there for a second, trying to catch my breath from all the frenzy. As I looked into the room, the headlights from the truck blinded me and I couldn't get a clear view. I moved my head around to avoid the brightness of the beams. I then stepped around to the side and noticed that the front of the truck was in the back of my living room.

The man still stood there, leaning casually on the driver's door. He had a blank look on his face as if to say, "Where am I and who are you?" I glanced above the pickup and saw that the whole inside wall of my bedroom was completely gone. The only thing left of that wall was one two-by-four piece of wood dangling from the ceiling where the bedroom doorway used to be. Behind the pickup the whole back brick wall of the bedroom was completely gone. Street lights glowed outside. The lingering, thick haze gave these lights an eerie, surreal look.

I slowly crept toward the truck and looked around in the rubble. This rubble used to be my outside bedroom wall and my inside wall, the wall that separated my bedroom from my dining room. I saw broken bricks, splintered wood, pieces of plaster board. Shattered glass reflected the headlights. Plywood. And sheetrock in the mix. It was all gathered up around the truck in a heap. My house was a complete mess.

My body began to tingle. I glanced underneath the truck. What in the world? There was a corner of our blue mattress. I looked closer and now I recognized the blue sheets. I leaned closer still and saw something moving underneath the truck—then it hit me! My eyes opened wide as it became apparent to me what had happened.

"God, *no!*" I shouted. "Ava's under the truck!"

I grabbed the truck and rocked it back and forth. I pushed. I lifted. Anything to move the truck off Ava. They say that sometimes in the heat of an emergency adrenaline runs so high that it gives you the strength of ten men. I felt as if I had that, but still I could not move the truck at all.

I screamed for the man to help me move it. He stood there and did nothing. I screamed out for anyone to help me. "Somebody, please help me move this truck! My wife is under this truck! Somebody, please help me save Ava! She's gotta be here. She's not anywhere else in the house. She's underneath this truck!"

My cries were in vain. I felt lonely and helpless. I stopped to catch my breath and looked at this man, puzzled about why he was still standing there and not helping me lift the truck. Then I heard banging on the front door. I ran to it and opened it up. In stepped an older black man. I had no idea who he was or why he was there. His eyes were filled with tears. They were hollow and transparent.

"Oh, my God," he cried. "I can't believe what just happened. I saw the whole thing happen."

I felt frozen and numb at that moment. Partially for him because I felt the emotion in his voice and from his face. And partially because it started to hit me—the impact of what he was saying, the desperation in his eyes. An icy chill ran through me, like a sudden north wind that cuts you to the quick. I saw him put his hands down on his knees as his head slumped in disbelief.

Not knowing what to do, I ran past him out the door and down the street, two houses down. I banged on the front door of our neighbor's home, screaming and yelling at the top of my lungs, for him, his wife, his family, somebody to come and help me lift the truck up off of Ava.

"*Help! Help!* Somebody please help me! My wife is under the truck! Help me, please! Somebody please help me! *Help! Help!*"

I ran through the neighborhood in my underwear, a bloody mess, yelling and screaming for help. I turned around and ran back to my house. As I turned, I saw flashing lights in front of my home. A small crowd had gathered. I couldn't make out the faces of anyone.

Two paramedics grabbed me from behind when I ran back into the house, something any boy from Brooklyn reacts to by instinct, and I struggled to tear loose. They took me into the front bedroom and laid me on a couch. I was frantic and hysterical. I begged them to forget about me and to attend to Ava. "I'll be all right. I think Ava's under the truck. My wife is under the truck! See if she's okay. Don't worry about me!"

"You're going be fine, sir. We have everything under control," one paramedic said. "We know where your wife is. Other paramedics are working with her. Just try to relax and calm down now for us, okay?" They kept assuring me that she was fine and everything was going to be all right.

"Call my wife's parents. They live close by. Let them know what's going on," I said.

"We'll call them soon. We need to take care of you," they reassured me. "We'll take care of Ava. It's going to be fine with both of you."

They talked about my injuries. Lacerations crisscrossed my face and burns covered different parts of my body. One injury startled me. "He has a broken left forearm," the shorter paramedic announced to the other.

"A broken arm?" I asked in disbelief. I had been trying to lift the truck and banging on a neighbor's door. "No way! I can't have a broken left forearm."

They assured me that I did. I then looked at my left arm and did a double take. It was swollen up to the size of a small watermelon. A deep indentation that looked like a tire mark and a tire burn, with something black and dark was visible on it. My arm went limp every time I tried to move it.

By this time my arm was throbbing, my face felt as if it were on fire, and my heart was racing at two hundred miles an hour. The paramedics continued to assure me that Ava was okay.

Then, strangely, out of nowhere, a Bible verse popped into my head. It was a scripture that I remember learning in my early childhood—the 23rd Psalm: "Yea, though I walk through the valley of the shadow of death, I will fear no evil. For thou art with me."

This verse rang in my heart and my spirit, and I didn't know where it was coming from. Was God telling me something? Was I about to die? Was Ava about to die? What was going on? My mind was racing. I didn't know what was going on. I lay there crying, praying, and wondering.

All of a sudden, they loaded me on a stretcher, carried me out the front bedroom, wheeled me past the people outside, put me in the ambulance, and closed the doors. *Somebody please wake me up from this bad dream*, I pleaded in my mind.

As the ambulance drove away, I saw the house. I saw the lights flashing, people gathered in front of the house, and what looked like a huge opening in the side wall where the bedroom had been. I saw our house in the distance getting smaller and smaller. I wondered, *What happened to me? Where is Ava? Is she okay? Will everything be fine? And what in the world is going on here?*

CHAPTER 7

THE TRUTH HURTS

On the way to the hospital I cried and prayed and asked questions about Ava. "Where's Ava? I want to see Ava. Can you tell me what's happening to her?" I asked in desperation to the paramedic leaning over me in the back of the ambulance. I spit more glass out of my mouth and coughed out thick blood. The paramedics didn't talk to me in any detail about Ava. They answered basic questions to calm me down, but didn't elaborate.

"We're attending to her. We know where she is," they said again. It was the same thing they told me in the house when I had asked earlier. I didn't like the feeling of being in limbo—of not knowing. It was starting to eat at me.

We arrived at Humana Clear Lake Hospital about ten minutes later, although it seemed like an eternity. My arm throbbed worse than ever. My face and body felt as if someone had set them on fire.

The doors opened and they wheeled me into the emergency room, then… they just left me there. They left me right there by myself. They must have known by this time that I was not in a life-or-death situation. I tried to calm down and began to come out of shock. I lay there in the hallway and saw the doctors and nurses talking about me in the distance. They would check on me every few minutes, then walk away and confer some more. All the while I was thinking, *What the heck is going on? One minute I'm saying goodnight to my wife, the next thing I know there's a truck in my house. Then I'm lying in a hospital emergency room, and nobody's telling me what's going on.* I knew sooner or later that I was going to wake up from this terrible dream.

I propped myself up as best I could. A few minutes passed. What's happening with Ava? Why isn't she here yet? Why isn't anybody telling me what's happening with her? I sat for a few more minutes. Dazed. Confused. In silence.

Then I saw a man walking toward me. He was wearing a gray jacket, black slacks, and a gray shirt with a little white collar at the top. As he stepped up to my bedside, I looked at him.

"Are you Bobby Petrocelli?" he asked.

"Yes."

He introduced himself as the chaplain of the League City Police Department. He was silent for several seconds. He swallowed hard. I saw a lifetime in his eyes as he fought back tears. I thought to myself, *How does this man know who I am? Does he know me from my being a local teacher? Do I coach one of his children? Has he seen me at Lakewood Church? How does he know my name?*

"Listen," I said. "I don't know why I'm here. I don't know where my wife is. Nobody's telling me anything. Do you know what's happening? Will somebody please call my wife's family? Here's their phone number. They only live ten minutes away. Please call them. And where is Ava? Is Ava okay?"

There was an awkward silence. He again swallowed hard. I felt his uneasiness. His lip quivered and his nostrils flared with the strain.

"I'm sorry to tell you... that you wife did not make it."

Didn't make it? Didn't make it? I said to him, "Oh, I see... Ava's still at the house. She'll be here in a few minutes. She's on her way to the hospital. That's what you're telling me, right?"

"No, Bobby. You're wife did not make it."

I thought for a split second and then answered back, "She's still in the ambulance—on the way to the hospital. That *is* what you're telling me, isn't it? Please tell me that's what you're saying!"

He hesitated for just a moment, then abruptly cut me off. He now spoke in a sharp, clear, no-nonsense tone. "No, Bobby. I'm sorry to tell you. Your wife did not make it. Your wife is dead."

I heard him that time. But I didn't say a word.

CHAPTER 8

AT THE HOSPITAL

Numb, that's what I felt.

My arm throbbed. My face was on fire. But I felt numb.

How could Ava be dead? Not more than two hours earlier I had come home and eaten a bowl of pasta that she had made.

Dead?

We had watched "The Honeymooners" together and cuddled in the chair.

Dead?

We had talked about Nicholas' birthday, my family coming down for Thanksgiving, going early Christmas shopping on Saturday. How could she be dead? I couldn't believe this was true. This was some kind of sick, cruel dream. I was going to wake up soon. I just knew I was going to wake up.

I guess you could say I was in shock. I guess you could say I was in denial. But one thing I couldn't deny—I would never get Ava back. She had been stolen from me like a thief in the night, snatched from my arms in my very own house. We couldn't have been more secure, could we? Asleep in our home. Locked up tight. A brick fortress around us. What could be safer than that? Yet somehow, it hadn't been enough.

The doctors didn't want to work on me until some family came to the hospital. I asked the chaplain to call the Dorsetts, and he did. Thinking about it now, I was upset with him for telling me that Ava was dead. I would rather the Dorsetts had told me. He told the Dorsetts on the phone that Ava had been fatally wounded and that I was in the hospital. There again, it would have been my preference for him to tell them in person rather than over the phone.

Mr. and Mrs. D. arrived shortly, and they were understandably hysterical. "Bobby, can you remember what happened? What happened, Bobby?" they asked with a frenzied desperation in their voice. They didn't know what had happened—whether we had been in a car accident or what.

Bit by bit I was getting sketchy details of what had happened. I tried to piece it all together myself, but I didn't have enough information. I lay there for what seemed like an eternity. My body was beginning to tingle and, in other places, flashes of extreme pain shot through me. Blood seeped through the bandages over the wounds. I could feel the open gashes in my face, my leg, and my arm—the one where the bone had been severed in half. I don't know what hurt more: the physical pain of my injuries or the pain of feeling defenseless against what had happened to me in my sleep.

The Dorsetts called some of our friends: Tommy and Rachel Birchfield, Saleim, and other friends from Lakewood Church. Soon they were at the hospital. The district attorney who had come out to the scene of the accident happened to be the father of one my students. He recognized my name from the police scanner, so by morning, all of Santa Fe knew. Many friends, faculty, students, and staff from Santa Fe High School began pouring into the hospital that morning.

When Bill Dorsett, Mr. Dorsett's brother, called my family in New York to tell them about the tragedy, my sister Debbie answered.

"Hello, is this the home of Debbie Pulzone?" Bill Dorsett asked in a quivering voice.

"Yes, this is she," Debbie replied on the other end.

"There's been an accident involving Bobby and Ava... "

Debbie screamed and dropped the phone. "*Ahhhhhhhhhhhh!*"

My brother-in-law Nicky picked up the phone after Debbie became hysterical. Bill explained to Nicky what had happened and when he repeated the news to Debbie, they both cried. Debbie told me later that this was one of the few times she had ever seen Nicky cry. This hurt ran deep. Debbie then passed the word onto my mother, who lived upstairs in the same house. The very next morning Debbie and my mother flew into Texas to be with me.

An hour later they stitched up my face. The hole in my right cheek was so big you could see my tongue through the side of it. They stitched up my right eye, and removed glass fragments from my face and slivers from my mouth.

"Mr. Petrocelli, can you sit up at all, sir?" one nurse asked. I shifted my weight and tried to sit up, but couldn't pull myself fully upright. Using a scrub brush they tried to remove the tar and rubber that had been burned into my right arm, my leg, my back, and my left forearm.

"*Ahhhhhhhhhhhhhhhh!*" I screamed at the pain.

"I know this is painful, but we have to try and clean you as best as possible before we dress your injuries, Mr. Petrocelli," another nurse said.

They scrubbed and scrubbed and scrubbed, but finally realized that they couldn't get much debris out and would need surgery to remove it completely. My left forearm was indeed broken, the bone severed cleanly in half. Not a pretty sight. They decided to put it in a temporary cast. "Bobby," the doctor told me, "we're going to have to do surgery and place a metal plate with screws in your arm to repair the bone and allow it to heal properly."

I lay in bed and tried to explain to Mr. and Mrs. Dorsett the sketchy details of what I knew about that evening. "All I remember was waking up, slumped over in the dining room. Then I looked up and saw a full-sized pickup in the living room and bedroom. Then a man stepped out of the side of the truck." Just as I mentioned this, the police walked by outside my open door—with the man. He was hand-cuffed and bandaged. He was being taken to jail after being treated.

Finally, I was taken upstairs to a private room. Tommy and Rachel were there with the Dorsetts. They prayed for me and tried to comfort me.

"Our most loving and merciful Heavenly Father. We come now into your presence—hurt, confused, not knowing what to say, not knowing what to do, not knowing why you've allowed this terrible tragedy to happen. We do know, O God, that you promised to never leave us or forsake us. We need to know that right now, God. We feel left and for-saken. Bobby needs to know that you love him as a father loves his son."

I didn't look up, but I could hear someone starting to cry.

And then another. And another.

I couldn't contain my grief any longer, and the tears flowed freely from my eyes. I shivered as a cold chill ran over my body. Then I was embraced, carefully, yet lovingly, by the warm and welcome arms of my mother- and father-in-law and their family. It was the first comfort I had felt since the ordeal had begun.

Before I knew it, from the pain, emotion, and exhaustion, I dozed off to sleep. Several hours later, someone's watch alarm went off. "Ava, that's the alarm. It's time to get up," I said. I looked around the room and that's when it really hit me. I was still in the hospital.

It was now Friday, October 25, 1985. I spent the entire day in the hospital. I continually received calls from family and friends around the country, some of whom told me they were coming to Texas, others who sent condolences. Many people from Lakewood Church, Santa Fe High School, and our community continued to arrive to be by my side. A wave of sympathy and love flooded my hospital room. I was engulfed in their outpouring of love and emotion for both Ava and myself. It was just what I needed at that time. I needed to know that someone loved me. I needed to feel their prayers and support lifting me up and interceding on my behalf.

That night, while lying in my hospital bed watching the ten o'clock news, I saw the lead story. The reporter said, "Just when you thought your house was the safest place to be, then all of a sudden something like this happens... " They showed the video of my house and reported that a truck had come crashing through my bedroom wall. The news reported that Ava had been killed and I had been treated and released from the hospital. I screamed at the T.V., "Oh, yeah. Then what am I doing here right now?"

I left the hospital on Saturday morning, knowing that I would have to return to have several surgeries performed, but, more importantly, knowing that I would have to bury Ava, my wife of only two and a half years. Even after all this, I still hoped and prayed that it was all a bad dream. I could only hope.

CHAPTER 9

REALITY HITS

Saturday morning, October 26, 1985. Mr. and Mrs. D. drove me back to their house from the hospital. As soon as I got out, my family and many friends from around the country came out to greet me. Tears welled up in my eyes and a huge lump grew in my throat as I saw those who had come to be by my side.

Many of them had dropped everything and come within hours of hearing of the tragedy. I felt the compassion and unashamedly open rush of emotion from each of them as I saw them for the first time, standing there in the Dorsetts' driveway. They were still twenty feet from me, but the magnetic force of God's love radiated from each one of their bodies, a knowing that they were there for me, that they believed in me, that they would do everything in their power to help me through this day—the first day out of the hospital. Jay and his wife Linda were there, Jakey, Riv and Cheeks, Ava's best friend Toni (Swain) Fowler, her family and little sister Alli, who had cystic fibrosis, and who was always so special to me.

I remember all of my friends' faces. They were so serious. Cheeks, who was always laughing and joking around, didn't crack a smile. Jakey, another crazy one from school, was unusually somber and quiet.

Craig Olson had come from Tulsa. Joe Liberatore and Chris Harrison, teammates of mine from the ORU baseball team, had dropped everything and driven down from school. It meant the world to me that they had taken the time to be there.

The Dorsetts' neighbors were out of town and let us use their house. Some stayed for a few days, others for a week.

The most humbling experience in my life was being bathed by my friends. I couldn't bathe myself due to my

injuries. You know you have true friends when they're willing to carry you and bathe you—even your most private
parts. I consider these friends closer than brothers. It took
them more than an hour to completely bathe me and wash
my hair. Jay, the strongest of the fellas, lifted me up and
held me while Riv washed my legs. Craig cleaned my arms.
Cheeks rinsed off the soap. Joe Lib and Chris washed my
back. Jakey shampooed and rinsed my hair.

Riv, Cheeks, and Jakey washed my bottom and my other
private parts. They all joked and rode each other about this,
but it needed to be done, so they did it. I'll never forget the
feeling of helplessness and the humiliation of not being
able to bathe myself. This was eased because I knew how
much these guys loved me as their brother. We had all been
through so much together back at school at ORU. I could
not have been in better hands.

It was a tremendously sad time for all of us, but despite
the pain we all felt, we were able to laugh a few times
together. Riv joked that my bottom needed to be cleaned
again and that Joe Lib would have to do it. Joe declined,
saying, "That's Cheeks' area of expertise."

"Jakey can fill in for me this time—I hate getting *behind*
in my work," Cheeks retorted.

We all had a good laugh. It reminded me of our old
times together. This is how I would normally be with these
guys—always joking and laughing. It felt good to laugh. It
felt good to be with so many friends who loved Ava and me
so dearly. I had had no idea how much they loved me, but
now I was finding out.

My friends finished cleaning me up. Day had turned into
evening. The fellas mentioned taking a ride and maybe stopping by the funeral home, and we crawled into the car and
left. Driving, driving, driving...

The weather was miserable. Hurricane Juan dumped tor-
rents of water on us and the rest of the Texas Gulf Coast.
We drove through the darkness, the rain, and the fog. I
remember being in the car and joking around like everything was okay and it was a normal, fun time. I remember
finally pulling up in front of this building. I remember they
had mentioned something about seeing Ava, but it didn't
register in my mind right away. Now Jay, Riv, Jakey, and
Cheeks got really quiet.

They opened the car door. I stepped out into the rain

and realized I was in front of Jack Rowe Funeral Home.

The Dorsetts waited inside the lobby. My friends quickly escorted me into the building and walked me through the foyer and up to a room with large, double doors. Jakey, Jay, Cheeks, and Riv walked me to the doors, opened them up, let me go inside, then backed out, leaving me in the room by myself.

Why were they leaving me inside this room all by myself? I didn't know why. I hobbled around slowly, using crutches because the truck had run over my leg and burned tar and rubber into my thigh. I stood there just inside the door for a moment to take in the complete area I was standing in at that moment. It was a long, deep room.

I started toward the front and could see in the distance a lavender casket with hundreds of flower arrangements around it. I limped closer to the casket. As I got closer I began to realize there was a female in the casket. Closer I hobbled. Closer, closer, closer...

There was no mistake about it. It was Ava.

All the while that this had been taking place, I had still thought in the back of my mind that it *must* be a dream. It had to be. How could all of this have happened so quickly?

I ran to Ava. I grabbed her and tried to lift her out of the casket. "Come on, Ava," I kept telling her. "We have to go home now. This dream must end. This can't really be happening. It's time to wake up."

The fellas rushed into the room and helped lay Ava back down. This wasn't a bad dream. It now finally started to set in. Like an anvil dropped on me from a second-story window, it hit me and nearly drove me into the pavement. Ava was not sleeping. It was now crystal clear: Ava was dead.

I had to come back to the funeral home the next day. All of my close friends and family were there. It was strange to see these people, most of whom normally would be cracking jokes and having a good time, being so somber and subdued. It was as if I were watching this all take place in some other person's life. I felt like an outsider looking in. Everything was eerily out of context. Out of place. Even my sister Debbie was mostly quiet.

That night, the night before the funeral, I went home depressed. Anguish and remorse gripped my heart. Love

and pain. Loneliness and fear. I didn't know what was going to happen in my life from this point. What would I do?
I didn't know. My whole life had changed drastically.

I tried to put up a front. I tried to be strong and show
everybody that I wouldn't let this get the best of me. I was a
fighter. A staggered, beaten-up fighter. I had barely gotten
up from the canvas before I was counted out. I had to
answer the bell. I had to go the distance. Even so, the pain
I had inside from losing Ava was more than I could bear. I
couldn't hide it. I broke down and wept several times, sometimes alone, sometimes with others. There was no way I
could keep it all bottled up inside. It hurt too much. It hurt
way too much.

Monday morning, October 28, 1985. The day of the funeral. It was another rainy, dreary day. My friends again
carried me and bathed me from head to toe. They dressed
me in a suit, doing the best that they could, trying to work
around my injuries. I rode in a limousine to Friendswood
United Methodist Church, where Ava and I had been married, and which now would be the site of her funeral service.
John and Dotie Osteen, from Lakewood Church, and Rever-
and Don Meador, from Friendswood United Methodist
Church, officiated at the service.

The pouring rain had not subsided for days. Arriving at
the church, I saw the water everywhere. There seemed to be
half a foot of it everywhere.

The limo pulled up to the front of the church and I got
out. As I entered the church, I saw it was packed. The church
normally seated about five hundred, and now almost two
thousand people were jammed into the sanctuary. For the
first time since the accident, as I walked into that packed
sanctuary, I cried tears of joy because I saw how much Ava
and I were loved. About eight hundred and fifty of the
people were students from my high school, and I felt an
overwhelming sense of love and affection from them being
there. I cannot describe the feeling of being rushed, mobbed,
and hugged by those hundreds of students. The looks on
their faces will live with me for the rest of my life.

For the first time, I realized why my life had been spared.
I knew when I saw their faces.

In the service, the Osteens gave the illustration of Moses

during one of Israel's battles. As the story goes, as long as Moses' arms were raised up, the Israelites would win. When he got tired and dropped his arms, they began to lose. The Osteens said that everyone as family and friends needed to be the ones to lift myself and the Dorsetts up in this time of need. We needed help to win this battle. We needed others to lift us up—to lift our hearts and spirits.

"Just as Moses needed his arms raised so that the Israelites would have victory, we ask you, O God, that you would help us to lift up Bobby's arms, the entire Dorsett family's arms, the Petrocelli family's arms—lift them up in victory, O Lord, that we might glorify you for your strength to overcome—just as you have overcome death—to give us life eternal. Amen and Amen."

After the service, I rode twenty miles in the pouring rain to Forest Park Lawndale Cemetery in Houston. An enormous line of cars followed. It took close to two hours to drive that twenty miles because of the driving rain and gusting winds.

We finally arrived at the cemetery. The pallbearers set the casket in place where Ava would be laid to rest. I watched this all from the limo, and when it came time, I stepped out of the solitude of the back seat into the wind- and rain-swept grass and mud, for a short service beside the grave. A small, green covering sheltered family members from the rain, and everyone tried to get under the tarp to keep dry. The benediction concluded, "Ava Dorsett Petrocelli has surely stepped into His glory, where she will live with Jesus forever, our Lord and Savior."

I turned to get back into the limo and, as I turned, I saw a thousand people standing in the rain. Every one of them was soaked. Few had umbrellas. This was the second time it became clear to me why my life had been spared. Of those thousand-plus people standing there in the pouring rain, once again I saw those eight hundred and fifty students from Santa Fe High School. Girls in high heels, mud up to their ankles. Boys in suits, soaked from head to toe. The rain didn't dampen their spirits. They were there for Coach Petrocelli. They loved me that much. It was truly a sight that touched me deep inside my heart, seeing those kids standing there as I drove away. My heart was full: full of love for the wife whom I had just laid to rest, and full of hope and tears for the young people whom I shall never forget paid me the highest tribute on that rainy afternoon at Forest Park Lawndale Cemetery.

This is an excerpt from an anonymous letter that I received following the funeral that day:

"What impact has this tragedy had on your life and on mine? Well, I just recently attended her funeral service. The rains and winds of Hurricane Juan had worked our community over for hours prior to Ava's funeral, and yet those forces could not stem the flow of people into the United Methodist Church. The church's parking lot was full and the paths to the church were under water, but that did not stop them either. They came with coats, with umbrellas, without coats, without umbrellas. They came in groups, and they came alone. Older people, younger people, teenagers, housewives, businessmen, church members, non-church members, Christians, and non-Christians. They came and they came. The church was filled, the hallways were filled, but most of all—their lives were filled by the spirit and the love for Bobby and Ava that I saw demonstrated that day. Their hair was wet and bedeviled by Hurricane Juan, their shoes oozed water, their clothing was mistreated and damp, but they were there.

I wish all of you reading this could have been there in that church also. To begin with, it was the first church service of any kind where I had to stand in line just to get in! And then, once inside, the task of moving around was even harder. There was a long line of people, mostly young people, filing steadily by the casket. It seemed an unending line.

As the service progressed and passages of scripture were read and songs were sung, the crowds in the foyer, who stood eight people deep, were solemn and reverent. Their hair was doused, their feet were soaked, their spirits were dampened, but they stood fast, and they stood quietly. They were as diverse a group as you could imagine, and yet they had a common bond—love. Yes, they loved Ava and they love Bobby, and the love that was throughout that solemn service was transferred. This love was so easy to see and even easier to feel. I am glad I was there to share that love. I am glad I knew Ava. So be like Bobby and be like Ava. Be good servants and increase your gifts tenfold, so that your life will be a light to all those in darkness.

Do not allow your tragedy to catch you in the dark without ever letting your light shine and shine and shine."

CHAPTER 10

SETTING IN

After the burial we returned to the Dorsetts' house. Our families and our closest friends were there to talk and have something to eat. Friends from all over the area had dropped off food for us. I was continually amazed by the outpouring of love and caring from so many people after the tragedy. When things like this happen it seems to bring out the best in people, with everyone forgetting about themselves and trying to be helpful in any way possible. With all the stories and news of everything bad happening in the world, this was something good. It strengthened my faith.

Most of my friends now had to return home, back to their different states, and back to their own lives. I was grateful that they had come to support me in my time of pain, but I knew that each one of them would eventually have to leave, and that I would be facing this fight without them.

Over the next few days after Ava's burial, infection started to set into my body. I tried for a few days to delay going back into the hospital, but my orthopedic surgeon ordered me to go in immediately to have the surgeries performed, before further problems could develop.

For two days prior to the surgeries, IVs with fluids and antibiotics fought the infections and flushed out the sickness that was invading my body. Jakey was with me. My mother and my sister Debbie were there. The Dorsetts also came to be with me.

Students from Santa Fe continually stopped by. From morning until night, students poured into the hospital in a constant stream. They took over the floor. They brought food, flowers, stuffed animals, candy, and cards. Some were special cards—rolled paper cards that reached more than a hundred feet long. They included signatures, sayings, greetings, and well wishes from every single student at Santa Fe High School. They had rolled out the sheets in the cafeteria at school where students, faculty, and staff had signed them. These are still special gifts that I have saved over the years.

This was the third time that I realized why my life was spared: to try and make a difference in the lives of young people.

The nurses on the fourth floor were incredible, allowing nonstop visitors, morning 'til night. They never made me abide by the visitors hours, which were supposed to end at ten o'clock each night. Though I had a semi-private room, no other patients were placed in there with me. The nurses did all they could to accommodate me. They were truly special. They realized that I was hurting both physically and emotionally. Again, actions spoke louder than words. I felt genuine concern and compassion from the nurses on my wing. It transcended what we would think of as "hospital care." It was nurturing and loving care that I felt from them constantly.

The next days were difficult. I had known the surgeries would be painful, but I had no idea how painful.

When the truck had crashed through the brick wall that night, the spinning tires burned into my body. Several times that week, several times each and every day, the physical therapist took me to the rehab room. He placed me in a whirlpool, with the purpose of loosening up the skin so that he could use tweezers to try and pluck the dead skin, the tar, and the rubber off my body. You know how painful a splinter in your hand is? Imagine a rubber splinter that has been burned into or even melted into your hand— that's what had happened to me, except both tar *and* rubber had been burned into my arm, my leg, my back, and my abdomen.

And these pieces were much larger than a little splinter. The PT kept plucking and plucking. Plucking and plucking. Deeper and deeper he dug. Constantly digging, digging, digging. This was nothing short of absolutely excruciating pain. It was torture.

"Bobby, if there were any other way I could remove the rubber and the tar, I would. You've got to believe me. The problem is, it's embedded and melted into your skin," the physical therapist told me for the fourth time that week.

Still, I soaked in the whirlpool. Then once my skin was soft, he would go to work on me.

"*Ahhhhhhhhhhhhhh,*" I would yell. He would stop momentarily—just long enough for me to stop screaming—then would continue until I screamed again. He would stop, I would fight the pain, scream, and then the whole cycle would begin again. I hated it.

Several times I almost passed out. I got dizzy from the combination of pain and fatigue from fighting the pain. I dreaded every minute. I would hate to see another person have to go through what I had to go through. After four days of this treatment, the PT finally determined that my case was too severe. He confirmed the doctor's diagnosis: the rubber had been seared into not only my skin, but seared into the muscles as well.

On my fourth day in the hospital, Dr. Boone repaired my left forearm with a bone graft from my hip. A steel plate was set in there also. In addition, surgeons removed the rubber and tar. Lucky me. The removal of the rubber left my body with a gaping hole in my upper right arm and right quadricep until the skin graft could be performed.

As I lay in the recovery room, I felt my arm throbbing again. It was a familiar feeling. The tar and rubber removal had been especially difficult, the doctor told me, because it had burned so deeply into my muscle. I now had to lie on my back for an entire week to recover, and strengthen myself for the next set of surgeries. Dr. Chin, the plastic surgeon, placed pig skin over the quadricep opening. Next up was a skin graft.

Seven long days I was laid up in that hospital room. Everyone was wonderful to me, but I had a lot of time to think. So for the next several days, that's what I did.

What am I going to do with my life now? I asked myself. *What's the next step?* A lot was going around in my head. The Dorsetts had made it clear that I was welcome to stay with them for as long as I needed. I could even stay until the following summer if need be. I didn't know if I should go back to teaching and coaching, move somewhere else, stay around the area... I wasn't sure. I had come to Texas primarily to be with Ava. Did I really have a reason to stay

here now? She had been my partner—my partner for life.
What kind of life was I going to have now? Was I going to
be alone for the rest of my life? Was that my destiny? To be
alone? I'm a firm believer that everything happens for a
reason. Somehow, there must be a reason...

"There must be a reason. There must be a reason. There
must be a reason...," I said. I searched and searched, but
found no reason. None anywhere. Like a blind man searching for a light switch in a darkened cave—that's how I felt.
I needed a bright ray of hope, but first I needed to regain
my sight. A cloud loomed over my head. I prayed that God
would bring sunshine back to my heart. The joy of my life
had been taken away, snatched from my very arms. My
heart felt as if a lead weight had been placed in it and I
couldn't move it by myself. I needed help from outside
sources—ones who would never leave me nor forsake me.
Sources who would stay with me forever.

Dr. Chin would have to remove skin from my inner right
quadricep and graft it to my right quadricep and right upper arm. I asked him to give me a saddle block—a long
needle in my spine to numb the lower part of my body. I
didn't want to be totally knocked out. I was emotionally
drained after the first set of surgeries and had a fear of being
put out again. He accommodated me. I watched as he used
a tool like a cheese slicer to remove the skin from the inner
part of my right thigh. Since I would have to be in bed for
an entire week of recovery, Dr. Chin did not want the skin
to be taken from my backside.

For the next week I was confined to bed, lying on my
back.

I had been in the Humana Clear Lake Hospital for nearly
three weeks, and now it was the day before Thanksgiving
and I was finally getting out of the hospital. Ah, Thanksgiving, usually my favorite holiday. A time for family to get
together and be thankful for blessings. I remembered that
my family was supposed to be coming down to visit Ava
and me and spend the holiday at our new home. Thanksgiving is a time to be grateful, and a lot of people tried their
best to tell me that I still had things to be thankful for. Did
I? Did I really? It's easy to be an onlooker and say that. But
they hadn't been through what I'd been through.

The story of my triumph over tragedy is one based on the foundations laid during my childhood, which held strong to bring me to where I am today. (Inset) My sister Debbie and I, during one of the few moments she wasn't getting me into trouble.

Mom, Debbie, and I (upper right) in Upstate New York with Beepa, Nanny, Roy, Billy, Aller and Uncle Artie (sitting). The summers in the Catskills were great times with my cousins. (Lower left) Mom and Dad, Attilio and Greta Petrocelli, when they first met.

The Petrocelli family in Brooklyn: Debbie, Mom, Dad, Chrissy, and me. (Lower) Dad, Mom, Debbie, and I with my father's parents, Attilio and Louise, at their 50th wedding anniversary.

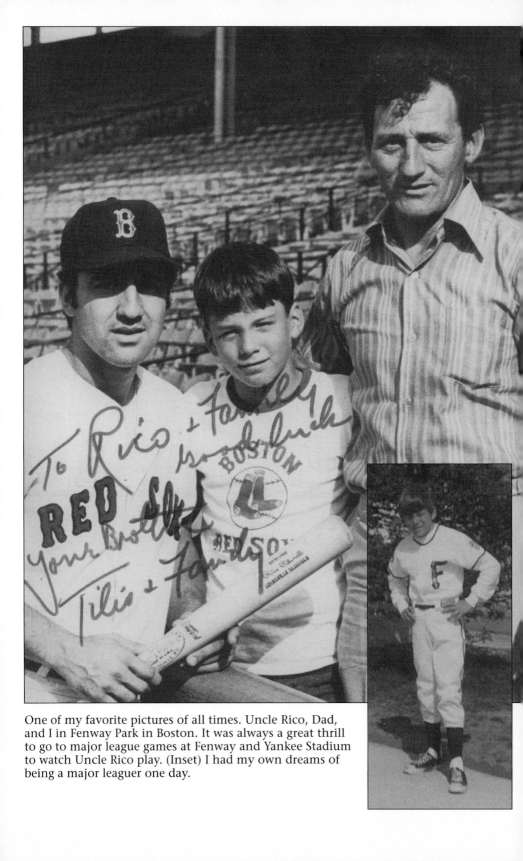

One of my favorite pictures of all times. Uncle Rico, Dad, and I in Fenway Park in Boston. It was always a great thrill to go to major league games at Fenway and Yankee Stadium to watch Uncle Rico play. (Inset) I had my own dreams of being a major leaguer one day.

Oral Roberts University in Tulsa, Oklahoma, where more friendships and foundations were established.

(Left) I fought for a spot on the Top 20 ranked Titans, but my baseball-playing days ended here with graduation.

(Lower right) The "fellas" – Cheeks, me, Riv, Jay, and Jake. Riv thought he was the Godfather.

Ava Lynn Dorsett Petrocelli, my Texas belle.

The Dorsetts and me: Randa, me, Ava, and Mr. and Mrs. D. (Linda and Randall).

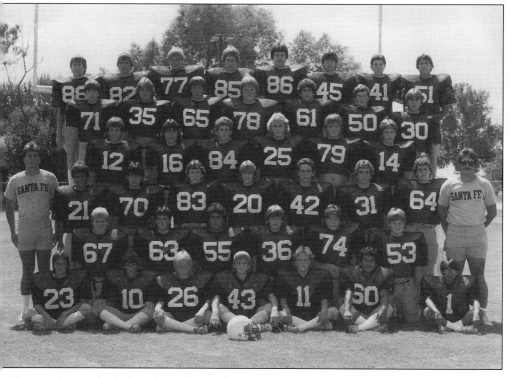

will never forget the kids at Santa Fe High School for their support. This is the freshman otball team I was coaching in the fall of 1985.

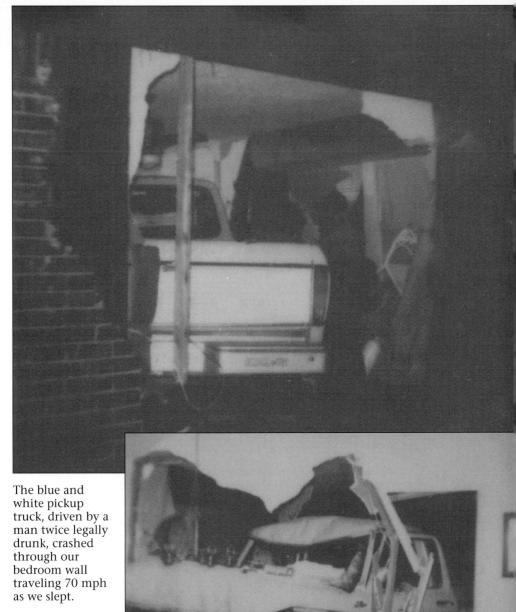

The blue and white pickup truck, driven by a man twice legally drunk, crashed through our bedroom wall traveling 70 mph as we slept.

All that remained of the wall between our bedroom and dining room was shattered sheetrock and a two-by-four with the smoke alarm. The window on the far left (bottom photo) was where I awoke that tragic night.

You can see where the tar and rubber had been burned into my right leg and arm. These pictures were taken about one week after the accident. The healed scars in the upper right photo are the same today.

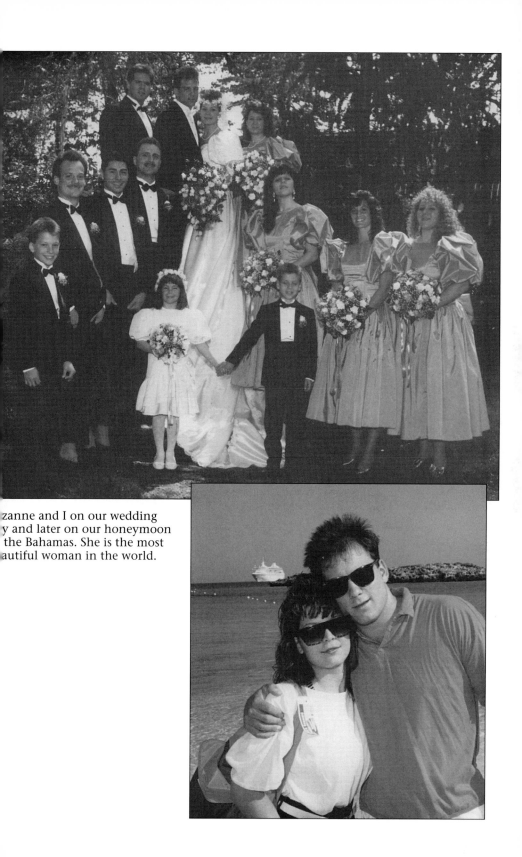

zanne and I on our wedding
y and later on our honeymoon
the Bahamas. She is the most
autiful woman in the world.

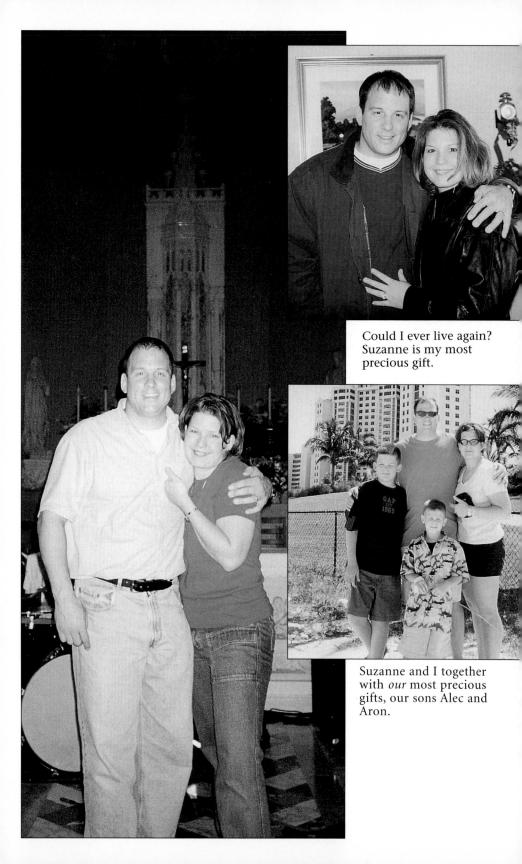

Could I ever live again? Suzanne is my most precious gift.

Suzanne and I together with *our* most precious gifts, our sons Alec and Aron.

dy's champs, Alec and Aron Petrocelli. They look just like their daddy.

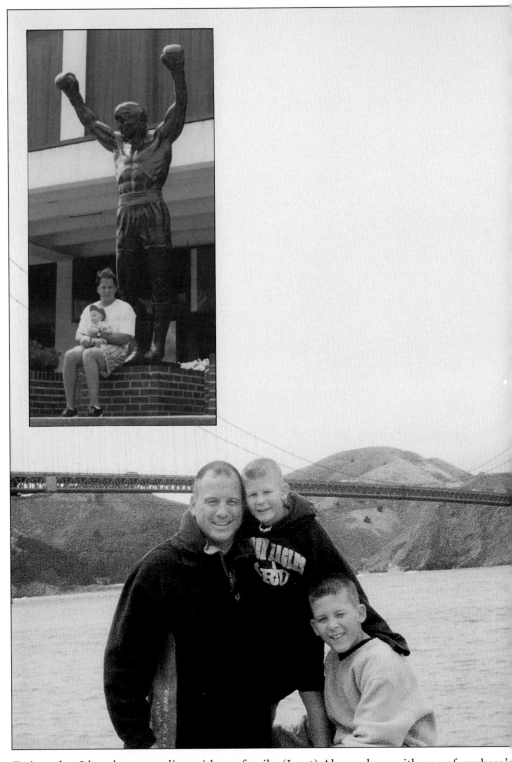

Doing what I love best, traveling with my family. (Inset) Alec and me with one of my hero's and inspirations, Rocky Balboa.

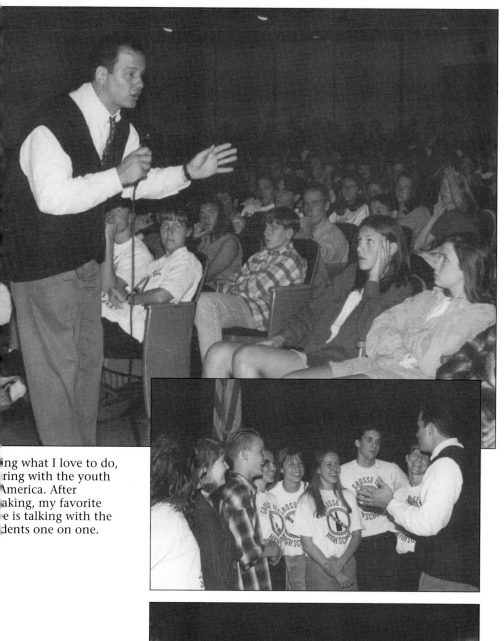

ing what I love to do,
ring with the youth
America. After
aking, my favorite
e is talking with the
dents one on one.

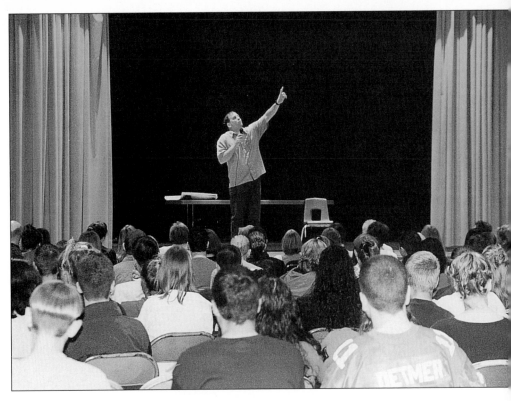

Ten seconds is all it takes to change a life forever. My desire is to reach as many youth as possible and persuade them of the importance of making responsible choices in their lives

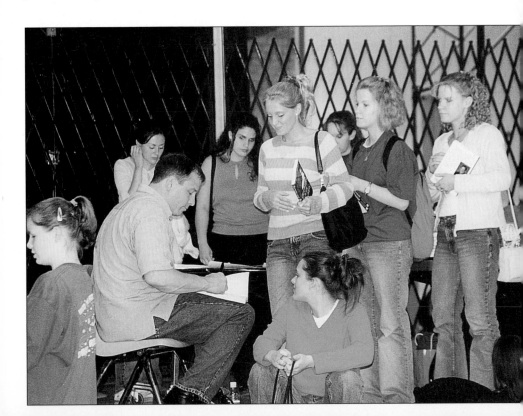

Does anybody really think they can feel what I've been feeling? I had done nothing to deserve this, yet my life was changed forever. I now had to start from Ground Zero. Could I piece my life back together? My wife had been taken from me. The future we had was gone. I had barely escaped with my own life. Was I supposed to put on a happy face and be grateful? It was hard to remember to be thankful. However, I was thankful that my injuries were not worse. I could've easily been in a worse condition.

CHAPTER 11

TEN SECONDS

In the car on the way to their home in Friendswood, a trillion thoughts raced through my mind, all at the same time. I was on my way back to the Dorsetts. Mr. and Mrs. D. had told me again that I was welcome to live with them for as long as I needed. I thought that was very generous of them.

During my three weeks in the hospital I had mostly watched television, listened to music and—most of all—thought. I had thought about this day. Today. When I would be riding in the car going to the Dorsetts'. I had thought about what I would do when I stepped into their home to live with them while I recuperated. I had thought about what I would say to Mr. D. when I first walked through the door. What could I say to Mrs. D. that wouldn't sound rehearsed? What could I say to Randa, Ava's younger sister, so as not to make it obvious that she would see me, but never her sister, again? I didn't know the answer to either of these questions. I didn't have a premeditated greeting for any of them. I just wanted to say what I felt. And what I felt was a lot of pain. I had lost my wife and that wife was their daughter. What can you say to that?

When I arrived at the house, Mr. D. was out running an errand. After driving me home, Mrs. D. began to work in the kitchen. Randa was at school.

I had thought about doing something a lot. It was something that was starting to eat at me really bad. So I did it. I was still on crutches, but I did it. I snuck into Mr. and Mrs. D.'s bedroom and got the keys to my 1983 maroon Toyota Celica GT. Mrs. D. figured out that I was going—she had that sixth sense. She knew.

She was quite upset that I was going to go—but I had to. I had to drive over to my house to see the entire scene. I had to go. There were no two ways about it. I absolutely had to see for myself. I needed to somehow figure out how all this could have happened. It was too crazy. Too far-fetched. Too much of a freak accident—though the word "accident" doesn't describe it. I had to see how a full-size pickup truck had ended up in the middle of my house.

The drive from Friendswood to League City, about seven miles, was especially painful. This was the exact route that Ava and I had driven countless times when returning from her parents home. The route was full of restaurants and stores and shopping places that we would go to all the time. I mean, all the time. I passed by some of our favorite places, places that had special memories and occasions attached to each one of them. I've heard that women don't forget things. I know a guy whose memory is pretty good, too.

I finally arrived in League City. The moment of truth was here. This was the first time I had returned to the house since the night of the tragedy. I was hoping to find some answers to the questions that were eating me up inside.

I slowly pulled into the entrance of our housing development. On the right side was the grassy field, Petro's Greens. I saw our house at the far end of it in the distance. It was weird looking at our house in this manner, like a stranger looking on from the outside, as if I had heard about some tragedy happening to other people and I wanted to see for myself. It was an odd feeling. A very odd feeling.

I slowed down and stopped short to get a full view. Tire tracks sliced across the grass field. They were straight and crisp, almost as if someone had drawn them with a straight-edge. They traveled on a beeline straight to the side wall of our house. The brick wall of our bedroom. The wall was completely gone, covered now by plastic and wood to keep out the rain. The plastic had since ripped and was blowing in the wind. It was a scary sight, looking at the house from the distance like this. It was off by itself, at the end of this piece of land, like a set from a movie.

Let me explain how our housing development was arranged. Our neighborhood complex sat off of road Farm to Market Road 518, the main street in League City. Two lanes came into the development and another two lanes exited. A divided median with trees and shrubs separated the two lanes going in from the ones going out. Our house was the first one on the right entering the grounds about a quarter of a mile in, at the end of the long, grass-covered field. This field was on the right as you turned in, and another grassy field mirrored it on the left. This property was eventually going to be used for shopping centers.

I looked at the skid marks on both sides of the median— the tracks going across the median, up over the curb, through the field, and directly to the house. This was insane. For someone to follow the path I was now looking at was unimaginable.

According to the police, at approximately 12:35 a.m. on Friday, October 25, eyewitness Jay Lane Ledbetter had been leaving the development. Jay reported that he had just dropped off a fellow worker, when he saw a light blue and white Ford F150 4x4 pickup truck enter the inbound lanes. The thirty-seven-year-old male truck driver swerved and fishtailed on the entrance road. Jay stated, "The truck gunned it—and really pushed it—coming in. I said to myself, 'Hey, if he doesn't slow down, something is going to happen.'"

A black Camaro pulled into the complex behind the pickup truck. The man driving the black Camaro was the same man who later banged on the front door of my house, telling me that he had seen the whole thing happen. Jay slowed down and watched. The truck, out of control, hit the concrete dividing median, went over the median, and into the two exiting lanes. It was now driving on the wrong side of the road for about thirty feet. Then, without warning, it crossed back over the median again, across the two incoming lanes. The full-size pickup then hit the curb and rode over it.

The truck sped across the grassy field, traveling 313 feet, which is more than the length of a football field. It proceeded on a direct path toward the brick wall on the side of the house. Judging by the distance, it was estimated that the truck was traveling 65 to 70 miles per hour when it crashed through the wall.

The truck crashed directly through our outside bedroom wall. The tire marks were so perfectly straight that it looked as if someone had purposefully driven into that area of the house. I said it before, but it was really weird. Really, really eerie and weird. It was as if the back wall had been a target.

I sat there and looked again at the skid marks, the tire marks, and the hole in the house where the wall used to be. When a car is going 60 mph, it is moving about 88 feet per second. For a car to be traveling 70 mph, it had to be moving more than 100 feet per second. That means, considering the length of the field and the speed that it was traveling, it took him about three seconds to come across the grass and crash through our brick wall.

As the truck crashed through the wall, it was airborne for an instant as a result of hitting the foundation slab of concrete under our home. I was sleeping about four feet from the wall. The truck landed on me and ran over me completely. The tires, spinning, burned rubber and tar into my body, then threw me up on top of the hood. It then carried me through the bedroom, past the inside bedroom wall, and threw me into the dining-room window at the back of the house, at which point my face shattered the window and I came to rest in a slumped position in the window. That's where I woke up, sitting in the dining-room window.

While I was riding on the hood of the truck, Ava was underneath being rolled up in the sheets and the mattress. As the truck continued through the house, Ava was being dragged underneath.

The truck plowed through our bedroom, through the wall between the bedroom and dining room, crashed through the dining-room table, and into the chairs that were in the back part of our living room. The front of the truck was now sitting in our living room after traveling about twenty five feet through the house. The cab was in the dining room. The tail end of the truck was in the back of our bedroom. Buried underneath the truck was Ava.

The paramedics later told us that when the truck hit her, it most likely knocked the air out of her body, then the sheets and the mattress wrapped around her face and body so tightly, she never got another breath of air. She died of asphyxia due to suffocation. The ironic thing is that she had no broken bones and hardly a mark on her body. But it had taken them twenty minutes to dig her out from underneath the rubble, and when they finally got to her, she was dead.

Now I sat in my car at the entrance of the development, thinking about all this, with the scene racing through my mind. I looked again at the skid marks and the perfectly grooved lines in the grass on the way toward the house. I visualized the truck crashing through the house, running over me and Ava, going through the inner bedroom wall, and ending up in the back part of our living room.

Two things started to dawn on me more than ever. First of all, this could have been prevented. Why? The man driving the three-quarter-ton pickup truck had a blood alcohol content of almost .20. It was actually .19. At this time in 1985, in Texas and in most states, to be considered legally drunk a person's blood alcohol level had to register a .10. (Presently, most states are moving to make .08 the legal level for intoxication.) So, therefore, he was considered double legally drunk.

I was told later that on that particular day, October 24, the driver of the pickup had had problems at his job and had gone to three different bars, drinking for most of the day. Then, after his final stop in a bar in Clear Lake, he had left, thinking that he could drive home. That's when he drove into my neighborhood, lost control of his vehicle, crashed through our home, killed Ava, severely injured me, and changed lives—including his own—forever.

I lost a wife. The Dorsetts lost a daughter. Randa lost a sister. Friends lost Ava. Aunts and uncles lost a niece. Even the drunk driver lost his family, since his wife and children eventually left him. And on top of this—my hospital bills totaled around $25,000. Tragedies are costly in every sense of the word. They take, and they don't give back.

The second thing that dawned on me, as I calculated the whole situation, was that this tragedy could not have taken more than ten seconds. *Ten seconds.* That's all it had taken for a foolish, irresponsible decision to be made. Ten seconds for a man to drive into our complex, lose control, hit the curb, cross the field, come through the wall, kill my wife, hurt me, and ruin our lives. Ten seconds! All of our hopes and dreams for a happy marriage and future together were taken from us in an instant—by a man who decided to drink and drive. Ten seconds. That's all it takes to change a life. Not a week. Not a day. Not an hour. Not even a minute. But ten seconds.

I sat there quietly for several minutes thinking about this as tears rolled down my face. It was a hard fact to swallow, that such a short time could have such a long impact.

I don't remember anything of the drive back to the Dorsetts. I can't even remember how long it took me. All I could think about was *that* ten seconds. My mind was too numb to think of anything else.

Ten seconds can change a life forever.

CHAPTER 12

WILL I EVER LIVE AGAIN?

The Dorsetts' house felt completely different to me now. This was to be my new home, at least temporarily, so I saw things with new eyes. I saw more detail. I paid attention to more of the little things around the house—the pictures on the refrigerator, the pattern on the wallpaper, the style of the furniture in the living room. It's like the difference between driving to someone's house one time and being a passenger the next time that you go to the same house. You pay more attention when you are the driver. The reality of being there was settling in. I had been there countless times visiting with Ava, but it was odd actually living there.

On the day before Thanksgiving, all kinds of thoughts were going through my head. Will I ever live again? Will I ever enjoy life again? Will I ever find happiness again? Will I ever experience joy? Can I enjoy going to the beach knowing what I look like now, after being disfigured? Will I have to go to movies by myself? Can I ever look at a sunset and not think of watching it with Ava? How will my time with her parents be? Can I enjoy the holidays at all?

I was lonely and anguished. I was stuck in a situation that I hadn't caused. I didn't deserve this. Why was this happening to me?

I thought about the kids at school. Would I go back to teaching and coaching at Santa Fe? What would my future hold? Should I stay in the League City area? Should I go back to New York? What was the right thing to do?

One bright ray of hope that day was Saleim, my close friend.

"Petro!" his voice said on the other end of the phone.

"Saleim, what are you up to, buddy?" I asked. Hearing his voice was a comfort in itself.

"Let's go see *Rocky 4* tonight."

"Sounds good, boss. What time do you want to go?" I asked excitedly.

Saleim was excited, too. I could tell by the tone of his voice. I'm a big Rocky fan and I was eager to see the newest film of the series. It was a good diversion for me, also, because I enjoyed being with Saleim and I needed to be able to temporarily escape from all the pain.

After the movie, we went to get something to eat. Saleim was my best buddy while living in the Houston area. He was athletic, a solid guy, and fun to be with. He reminded me of a lot of my buddies from college. He could have been one of "the boys." Saleim worked at Houston Baptist University and, while I had been in the hospital, had driven more than a hundred miles every night to hang out with me. He would leave straight from work and oftentimes would stay until past midnight, then drive back. That's a dedicated friend. I liked it when he came and took me away from the hospital. It was an escape, even if just for a few hours. I didn't have to stay in my room. I didn't have to dwell on why I was in the hospital in the first place—and I was not all alone.

I woke up early on Thanksgiving Day. Mr. and Mrs. D., Randa, and I were driving up to Palestine in East Texas to spend the holiday with Grandma Dorsett. Sitting in the back seat with Randa for the three-hour drive became awkward, and I tried to joke around and make the trip seem a little shorter.

But everyone in the car was thinking the same thing: Thanksgiving is supposed to be a time to be happy and thankful. How could we hide the fact that we hurt so much inside? I knew it was painful for the Dorsetts to drive all the way there with me, happy in one sense to have a son-in-law, but grieving over losing their oldest daughter.

Throughout the journey I thought of Ava. None of us could look each other in the eye for too long. We each cried out in our own way, looking for some reason this had taken place. The answers were not coming. We hoped someday they would.

Grandma Dorsett had cooked up a tremendous spread of food: turkey, stuffing, potatoes, greens, cranberries, cornbread—the works. We sat around the table anticipating the home-cooked feast. When she emerged from the kitchen carrying the turkey, however, her eyes fell on the empty chair where Ava would have sat, and we all momentarily stared silently at it. Her happiness quickly dissipated. She mustered up a false smile, but it was as empty as the chair.

We tried to enjoy the food, but the chair sat empty, a reminder of Ava. In past years by this time we would have been talking and laughing at stories that Grandma told about Mr. D. and his childhood. There were no stories this year. There was very little talking. No one knew what to say. Most questions were answered with a nod of the head or a quick glance in that person's direction. Most of the time, none of us made eye contact. We didn't want to see the pain and sorrow that filled each of our hearts, the pain that was mirrored in our eyes and that shook our very souls.

"So, Randall, how's business going?" Grandma asked. Mr. D. just nodded without looking up or speaking a word. The rest of us stared at our plates and ate. We mostly looked at each other with our peripheral vision—never looking directly at each other at all.

The silence and awkwardness was so staggering that I got up from the table several times and went into the bedroom—and cried. I couldn't get over the fact that she wasn't there. This Thanksgiving happened to be my twenty-fifth birthday. November 28th. How could I have a happy birthday? I was a quarter of a century old, and in immense pain.

I decided that I would return to teaching at Santa Fe High School after the Thanksgiving break, so I notified the school. I had mixed feelings about the decision because I didn't know how I would react to being with the kids again. Could I face the kids? Could I look at them? Could I enjoy teaching as I had before? I knew this was probably the best thing to do, to get back into spending time with the kids and to get my mind off the tragedy. I had to move forward with my life. Physically, I had recovered well enough to resume my teaching duties.

I was nervous that first day back because I didn't know how I would react to seeing the kids again. I was so touched that they had supported me throughout the whole time, at the funeral in the pouring rain, at the cemetery in the mud, and at the hospital while I was recovering. What could I say to them? Would I break down and cry? How would my first day go?

The drive to school on December 2, my first day back since the tragedy, was long. Each minute seemed like an eternity. When I pulled into the parking lot, I sat in the car for a few moments before opening the door to get out. I still had doubts about trying to come back.

A few students saw me as I got out of the car. "Coach Petro's back. Coach Petro's back," I heard them say in the distance. For an instant I thought that I should act as if I hadn't heard them, but instead I waved and gave them the thumbs-up sign. They hesitated, staring at me, not knowing how to respond. Then they mimicked me and gave me a thumbs-up.

I felt as if everyone's eyes were glued on me as I walked into the building, and they probably were. I don't know if they were in disbelief, or shocked to see me walking the halls again. Chills and goose bumps ran through me from the feeling of being in Santa Fe High School again, as if I were a stranger everyone knew. It was an odd sensation.

The students' eyes filled with tears when I walked into my first class that morning. I remember the uncertainty on their faces. They didn't know how to react. A lot of them cried and were full of emotion. I, too, had tears in my eyes each class that first day. I was happy to see the kids because I loved them so much and, by the same token, I knew that they loved me. It was an emotional first two weeks back, but I tried my best to be strong for the kids and not show too much emotion.

But, every day for months, I cried the whole way back to the Dorsetts', because I knew Ava would not be waiting for me.

As best as I could, I tried to get back into a routine. I needed to take my mind off the loneliness. I needed to keep busy with positive things, instead of dwelling on my own hurt and sorrow.

Christmas was coming. I saw the decorations everywhere. I heard Christmas carols on the radio and in all the stores. The malls were buzzing with Christmas spirit.

I had to do my Christmas shopping. The family helped with most of it because I wasn't in any mood to do it by myself. I kept thinking about the stores Ava would go to. Ava had already picked out a sweater, a shirt, and a bottle of Paco Rabanne cologne for me. I wouldn't be able to pick anything out for her.

I had loved to buy her things. She always lit up like a child when I brought her presents. In her absence, I just couldn't get into the Christmas spirit. I had no holiday cheer, no sense of anticipation or excitement, knowing that— without her—it would all be fake happiness.

I flew to New York to spend Christmas in Brooklyn with my family. Everybody says there's no place like New York for the holidays. Usually I would agree, but I could've been anywhere in the world that year, and it wouldn't have made a difference. Without Ava, it was going to be a difficult holiday.

My family tried their best to cheer me up on Christmas Eve and make it happy for me. I felt bad for them because they tried so hard not to mention things that would remind me of Ava. Christmas Day wasn't much better. Despite the fact that we were all together and had each other, they knew I was hurting, and they hurt with me. Sometimes love hurts.

I called Mr. and Mrs. D. on Christmas Day. They were at Meemaw's house in Kingwood, and I could tell it was a somber Christmas for them, too. They said they had gone to the cemetery earlier to visit Ava's grave. I had gone to the cemetery a lot myself. I went on weekdays, weekends, all the time. I put flowers on her grave and talked to her, asking her why she had left me alone.

New Year's Day 1986 came and went in New York without much fanfare. I felt like a nomad that day, a wanderer. Wandering from house to house, spending time with different friends and families, not really feeling comfortable anywhere, but going just the same. It was an empty feeling. I didn't belong anywhere I went. Everyone tried hard, but I had a hollow, empty feeling of loneliness. It's one thing to be lonely and be by yourself. It's worse to be with a lot of people and still feel lonely.

The next months were lonely ones, indeed. I went to the mall by myself. I watched couples walk hand in hand as Ava and I had used to do. It hurt to watch so many happy couples together. Where was my happiness? No one was holding my hand. No one was walking with me. I ate in the food court—by myself. I visited our favorite restaurants—by myself: Casa Ole, El Chico's, and many of the other Mexican restaurants that we loved so well. I went to the stores we had frequented: Target, Miller's Outpost, The Gap, Sam's Club, the Christian music and book stores.

For the first time since we had been married, I was going to all of these places alone. We had loved to stop by Chick-Fil-A for a chicken sandwich and waffle fries. We had loved going to the beach, even in the wintertime. We had taken rides down to Galveston to enjoy the peace and quiet of the water. As we walked along the shore, the sun would just be coming up over the Gulf of Mexico, the waves would be crashing and the sea gulls hovering for food, squawking and carrying on.

Going to church was difficult, also, so I went infrequently. I was confused, hurt, angry, and frustrated. Confused that God had allowed this to happen. Hurt that I was now alone and having to start over. Angry because I had done nothing to deserve this kind of tragedy. And frustrated that I was in a situation that I had no control over. Ava and I had been active with the youth in our church. Seeing the young people and other church friends only reminded me of her; and of the wonderful times we had spent there.

I was experiencing the biggest rollercoaster of emotions in my life. I did things to try to find happiness, then searched again for something else to help me through the next period of loneliness. Some people say that grief is a day-by-day experience. It wasn't like that for me. It wasn't even a minute-by-minute kind of thing. For me it was a second-by-second battle to try and understand why this had happened to me. I constantly wondered if I was going to continue with my life. The thought, *Will I ever live again?* kept playing in my head.

I kept a journal of my feelings and thoughts. Valentine's Day in 1986 was an emotional day. While others were celebrating the joys of love in their lives, my love was dead. How could I enjoy this Valentine's Day? I wrote these words later, on February 25, 1986:

"Today marks four months since my baby has gone. The hurt becomes more real with each passing day. God, help me to find acceptance in this crazy situation. My love for Ava is greater than ever, though I don't have her here with me. God, ease this pain that is so physical in nature. Comfort me in this time of loneliness. Since Valentine's Day, the pain has been sharper. Why, God, has she gone away? Was it my fault? Please be so real to me, for I need you more than ever.

"Today was such a beautiful day. The beginning of Spring is so evident. These were special times for me and Ava. Lord, as Spring brings forth such natural beauty (since Winter cold is ending), please let your beauty illuminate me during this time of anguish. Help me, Lord, for I truly love you. I picked this book [my journal] because of the beauty it displays [a beach scene on the cover]. We truly loved the beach. Oh, how I miss being on the beach with her. The tears roll down my face—they pour from my heart. God, have you betrayed me? Why am I deserted and left alone? I need you, Lord."

The toughest times were at night. I couldn't sleep. I began to have panic and anxiety attacks. I would wake up in a cold sweat, my heart pounding so hard that I thought I would have a heart attack. This scared me because I thought I was too young to have heart problems. I didn't understand what was going on. I did realize that, emotionally and psychologically, it was an uphill battle.

Each one of us was going through many of the same feelings. Mr. D., Mrs. D., and Randa were all feeling anguish, doubt, anger, and guilt. Whenever a tragedy like this happens, it's natural for everyone close to that person to feel a sense of responsibility. "What did I do to cause this to happen to Ava?" "How could I have prevented this tragedy?" "Should we have moved into the house in the first place?" "Why is this happening to our family?" Each one of us wanted answers. None of us could understand why.

On March 12, 1986, I reached my lowest point. It would have been our third wedding anniversary. I had been keeping a calendar of days since Ava's death and knew the exact number of days—the hours—even down to the minute. When I arrived at the cemetery to celebrate our anniversary, four months, fifteen days, fourteen hours, and twenty-five minutes had passed since Ava had died.

I sat in the car and didn't get out. I yelled from the distance at her grave. Slowly, I walked to her burial place. I stood over her grave and stared at her name on the tombstone and the epitaph that read, "She touched her world for Jesus." After a few minutes I placed a bouquet of yellow and purple irises on the stone, right over the date that she died.

This was the day I felt the greatest degree of loneliness, despair, anguish, and hurt. Though I believed she was in a better place, the pain was still excruciating—I missed her more than words can say. She was not only my wife, she was my best friend. Since October 25, this day was the worst of the worst.

I wondered if I would ever experience joy again. Real, honest, deep down joy. The kind that makes you feel strong inside. The joy that wells up from your soul and springs forth like a fountain.

CHAPTER 13

BEGINNING TO SEE THE LIGHT

It became increasingly evident that it would take a long time to work through my grief for the healing to take place. I would have to take it ten seconds at a time, minute by minute, day by day, week by week.

One phone call during my bleakest period really helped me. It came from Nancy Pearson, a friend from Oral Roberts University who now taught in the Houston area. Nancy had been at the wedding, and she had been to the funeral.

"Bobby, I've known you for a while, since 1980," she said. "You have always been someone whom I and many other people looked to as somebody with a lot of strength, somebody with a lot of confidence, a strong faith, a lot of joy—someone who so obviously loves to live. You care about life. You enjoy life. You live life to the fullest. You were always there for others and always listened to others. You are somebody who was always strong for other people."

Then she said, "Bobby, stop it! You've been trying to put on an act. You're trying to be strong for everybody—trying to show everyone that this is not going to get you down, that this is not going to destroy you. And I believe you are going to make it through this, Bobby. But we know you are hurting, we know you're in pain. *Let us help you. Let us strengthen you.* Just like the pastor said at the funeral, we want to uphold *you*, we want to hold up *your* arms, we want to strengthen *you* through this situation... "

When Nancy shared that with me, a burden was lifted. She was right. I didn't have to try and pretend that I was strong. I didn't have to keep up the façade that this wasn't going to get the best of me. I was now free to be honest with people and let them know that, yes, I hurt, yes, I was discouraged, yes, I needed my arms lifted for me, and yes, I needed to vent my emotions. I no longer had to be afraid to discuss my problems with people. I now felt a freedom and a release that I, in fact, had a choice in deciding which direction this tragedy was going to go. Was I going to let this tragedy get the best of me? Or was I going to get the best of this tragedy?

I now saw that it was my choice.

That call from Nancy was the turning point in my dealing realistically with Ava's death. The conversation triggered in my memory principles that I had learned while taking graduate courses in counseling and psychology at the University of Houston. These principals had been introduced by Elizabeth Kubler Ross in her book *On Death and Dying*. It suddenly hit me that I had been going through all of the stages of grief: denial, anger, shock, depression, bargaining, and acceptance—all except one.

I was in denial, because both shock and refusal to accept the fact that the tragedy had taken place had settled in. I was angry with Ava for deserting me, at God for taking her away, and at myself for things that I could've or should've done. I bargained with God, saying, "If you'll bring her back, then I'll... " Guilt ran through my veins: What had I done wrong to cause this to happen? Depression came like a blanket of darkness, in that I was extremely lonely when the reality that she was really gone set in.

I slipped in and out of each stage—except for the one termed "acceptance." It was now time for me to start a new beginning. My healing only began when I accepted that she wasn't coming back. I said "Goodbye" to Ava, and started anew.

This was a critical part of the healing process. I now knew that it was all right to talk about my true feelings. I could share with people how much pain I had gone through in the various surgeries. I could talk about Ava and what she meant to me. I went to the cemetery and to other secluded places and vented my anger—often yelling and screaming at the top of my lungs. I expressed to God my hurt, my confusion, and my pain.

I was no longer afraid to cry if I felt I needed to. This was a real release for me. Just as Nancy had said, I didn't need to pretend to be strong for anyone. I felt like crying, I needed to cry, so I cried.

I read articles and literature about death. It was a comfort to get different perspectives from other people who had been traumatized by a death. Andre Thornton, a professional baseball player with the Cleveland Indians, tragically had lost his wife and daughter in a van accident. Reading about how Andre dealt with his loss, trusted in his faith, and battled his way through, inspired me. I read about Dave Roever, a Navy Seal in the Vietnam War. A phosphorous grenade had blown up in his hand. He lived through it, but was severely injured. He fought back and has impacted many lives.

Another person who inspired me was Terry Law. Terry started a ministry called "Living Sound." Living Sound worked abroad, traveling throughout Russia and other parts of the world sharing love, hope, and God with people who desperately needed it. While Terry was in Europe with his organization, his wife was killed in an automobile accident here in the United States. Reading about how he dealt with his loss helped me to identify with someone who had gone through something similar to what I was experiencing.

Instead of going to a particular counselor, I was able to vent my feelings with family and close friends. My friend Jay, who was working on his master's degree in counseling and psychology, helped me recognize the things that I needed to deal with. The longer that time went on, the easier it was for me to move forward in a positive direction. I was no longer afraid to spend time alone. I didn't like it, but it didn't eat at me as much now.

I kept some special things of Ava's so that I could remember the good times and not try to act as if they didn't still mean a lot to me. I kept her wedding ring, her watch, earrings, clothing, and pictures. I also kept myself busy, especially with my students.

I volunteered with youth organizations like Students Against Drunk Driving and the Fellowship of Christian Athletes group, which I sponsored at Santa Fe. I spent more time with the kids individually and in small groups, taking them to ball games, concerts, and other activities that we had fun doing together. I knew that I had been spared so that I could someday share with young people about the dangers of drinking and driving.

I started to exercise and feel better about myself. I still felt self-conscious about my numerous scars and the permanent blemishes on my body, but I was getting back into shape and feeling more confident about my appearance. I also recorded my feelings and frustrations in the journal. This helped me to have an outlet for what I was dealing with on a regular basis. Finally, I had to turn my grief into creative energy by helping others.

I looked at life differently now. I had a new perspective. I knew that I had been spared for a reason. I could have been in a wheelchair. I could have had brain damage. I could have been injured worse than I was. Yes, I had had difficult surgeries, and yes, I had been severely injured, but it could've been much worse. I now had learned to look at the positive aspects of my circumstances instead of dwelling on the negatives and letting them weigh me down and keep me down.

I learned the importance of a little thing called attitude. I realized more than ever that I had the power to change that attitude and develop a positive outlook. I began to listen to uplifting and positive music. I started watching more comedies on television. I watched "I Love Lucy," "Abbott and Costello," and "The Little Rascals." This influx of comedy and funny programs helped to bring joy back to my life. I had learned how to laugh again. Just months earlier, I hadn't been sure if I would be able to.

Venting my emotions was so important. Whether it was talking, crying, praying, shouting, laughing, singing, praising, rejoicing, or whatever—I had to get my emotions out in any way I could. Sometimes I did all of the above, one right after the other. It gave me a needed sense of release. There were too many different feelings that I had to get out of my system. It was wonderful to be free enough to just let go.

One way I was able to experience a sense of release was by watching *Rocky* films, starring Sylvester Stallone. The original *Rocky* had always been one of my favorite movies. It's the story of a boxer, Rocky Balboa, a loser from the streets of Philadelphia who gets a once-in-a-lifetime shot at the heavyweight championship. He goes the distance with the champion and never gives up. Despite all kinds of adversity and hardship, Rocky triumphs over impossible odds. I identified with Rocky because he was just a down and out guy, fighting for his life.

I realized more than ever after talking to Nancy that I was going to have to make a choice. This situation was either going to make me a better person, or it was going to make me a bitter person. I had to go on and share all my feelings. I had to go ahead and let my foundation kick in.

One film that came out several years after Ava's death really hit home with me. *The Money Pit,* starring Shelley Long and Tom Hanks, is about an engaged couple fixing up an old home to move into when they are married. As the story goes, the house completely falls apart. The bathtub crashes through the floor, the fireplace collapses, the staircase breaks, the walls come apart, the electrical and plumbing systems are a complete mess. It's a comedy and it's funny.

But as the movie goes on, the couple's relationship also comes apart. As they are on the verge of splitting up, the contractor—who has fixed the home so that it is absolutely gorgeous—walks down the staircase he's just finished. Tom Hanks is on one side of the foyer and Shelley Long is on the other. The contractor, who is all too aware of their differences, lays the key to the house on the banister and asks, "Who gets the key?" He continues by telling them he had doubts whether the house could be fixed, but in the end he knew that it could because it had a strong foundation. He says that no matter how bad a house may be, if it has a strong foundation then it can be fixed. Then he said he knew their relationship had a strong foundation, and he left.

That struck me—the strong foundation. No matter what happens, no matter how bad, how bleak, how dark, how desolate a situation may seem—it can always be put back together if there is a strong foundation.

This was reaffirmed to me after witnessing the devastation left by Hurricane Andrew in Miami in August 1992. A three-day cruise turned into a five-day adventure because our ship could not sail into the Miami port during the storm. When we finally returned, the destruction was catastrophic; total housing areas lay in ruin and lives were left in chaos. The only thing left intact in the midst of the devastation were row after row of concrete foundations from each flattened house. I realized then that no matter how much destruction the storm had caused, the homes could be rebuilt on that solid foundation. If our foundations in life are strong, then even when the hurricanes of life come calling, our foundation will be left intact and we can always rebuild our lives.

We have to either rely on a strong foundation, rebuild a poor foundation, or start building a new foundation. My life, too, could be put back together if I stuck with my foundation—My "Five Fs": faith, forgiveness, family and friends, the willingness to fight, and feeding my total body good things.

CHAPTER 14

FAITH

Building a strong foundation comes down to making one choice, one decision at a time. This takes place one situation at a time: Brick by brick, row by row, layer by layer—one ten-second decision at a time, whether it's a good decision or a bad decision. That's how we build our foundation. The point we're at right now in our lives was reached by making one ten-second decision at a time. The pattern has been set little by little. Our habits influence our personalities and also our lives.

Faith was established in my life when I was very young. My family attended church regularly, and I learned Christian principles. From those principles, I became interested in a Christian university. It was a step-by-step progression, an outgrowth of what I had been taught when I was a child. The formative years in children are perhaps the most important ones in our lives. Those are the years that can determine the path our lives will take. Will we follow a right path? Or will we follow another path? The establishment of faith in my life had been an important element in my formative years.

There are two kinds of faith: first, a faith in a Supreme Being, a faith in a religion, a faith in God. My faith was very strong in my relationship with Jesus Christ. Second, the faith to believe in yourself, to believe that, somehow, some way, you can work to make the best of every situation and that you will ultimately get the best of it. Therefore, when I was faced with this tragedy, I had to rely on my faith.

A tragedy can steer people in two directions: it can control us, or we can control *it*. We have to make the conscious choice to have faith. Once we recognize that we have the power to choose the right path, then we can make the choice to be on the way to a better life.

I define faith in such a case by rejecting the norm. The norm would say, "This has happened to you, so you're going to have to be bitter, you're going to have to be hateful, you must be unforgiving, you must not be loving." Well, I had to choose to reject those negative feelings from the start. I had to choose to go against what many expected to see. I would not let myself buckle under the pressure of grief.

The second part of my faith is a knowing, that somehow I would make it through this situation. Even in the dictionary, faith is defined as "a belief without evidence, and a confidence in, or dependence on a person; belief in God."

I relied on a strong religious faith, knowing deep down in my spirit that no matter how difficult things might seem, no matter how tragic that the circumstances might be, I was going to make it through.

I knew God would always make a way. He says to "cast all your cares upon Him; for He careth for you" (I Peter 5:7). The whole Christian faith and belief system is not built on what society says and does, but on a belief that God will be our help. He will meet our every need. We have to do our part, but we also have to make the choice to allow Him to work through us and in us. He won't force himself on us. We must invite Him in.

Jesus overcame sin. He overcame adversity. He overcame temptation. But most of all, He overcame death itself—the ultimate adversity. If we believe that He overcame death, then why can't we believe that He will help us overcome anything that stands in our way? He wants to help us—and He will. All we have to do is ask and believe. He is ready and willing to be with us every step of the way, but first we have to recognize that we need His help.

I also believe that "faith without works is dead" (James 2:26). In other words, are we willing to put our money where our mouths are? It's easy to follow God and do what's right when things are going well, but what happens when things go wrong or we face difficulties? Will we just lie down and give up? This was a time that I had to stand strong in my foundation. This was a situation that truly defined my faith. I had to believe that faith in God would see me through.

People have asked me, "Don't you think that God could've steered the truck six inches to the left or six inches to the right? That way the accident would not have been fatal." It's probably true that the truck's impact six inches one way or the other would have meant a difference in life and death for Ava. But that did not happen.

The driver of the pickup made a choice. Then he chose to drink. He chose to drive. In the ten seconds it took for him to lose control of his truck, my life was changed, my wife's life was taken, his life was changed—all because he made the wrong choice. He had reacted from the foundations he had laid for himself.

There's an expression, "Actions speak louder than words." It's true. What you do speaks louder than any words you can ever say. I could've said, "Yes, I believe that God will help me through this," then sat back and done nothing. Or I could've said, "Yes, God will help me through this," and got out there and moved forward with my life and *allowed* Him to work through what I was doing. That's what I chose.

I get angry with people who sit around and mope, saying, "I need direction. I need guidance. God needs to tell me what to do next." Then they sit around, do nothing, and expect God to speak audibly to them about what their next move should be. I don't believe God works that way. If we don't know what to do next, we should get out and start doing things that we think He wants us to do. He'll make it clear one way or the other which direction He wants us to go. We make the choice, then God directs our path. Take that first step. Choose to have faith.

I heard a story of a man whose house was flooded in a rainstorm. This man got on top of his roof to wait out the storm and avoid the rising waters. A short time later a man in a four-wheel-drive vehicle came by and yelled up to him. "Sir, come down. We're here to rescue you." The man on the roof called down, "Thanks, but I'll be all right. God will take care of me. He will deliver me." So the vehicle drove off and left him.

A few hours later, when the water was so high that no cars could pass, a man in a boat came by. "Hey, mister. Get in the boat. I'm here to rescue you." The man on the roof said, "No. God's going to rescue me." The man in the boat looked puzzled, but moved on.

Later in the afternoon, the flood waters rose so high that they reached the man's roof. A helicopter flew over, the pilot dropped a ladder, and spoke through the loudspeaker.

"Hey, you on the roof. Grab the ladder. I'm here to rescue you."

"Oh, no. Thanks, anyway. I'll stay here. I'm trusting in God. He's going to rescue me," the man said. The helicopter pilot reluctantly left. The water rose again and the man on the roof drowned. When he arrived in Heaven, he asked God, "What happened? I trusted you. I had faith. Why did you let me drown?"

God said, "Save you? I sent you a Jeep, a boat, and a helicopter to rescue you. You were too busy thinking I was going to move and meet your needs in a certain way, instead of realizing that I was setting a way of escape for you!"

God provides different ways of escape for us. They may not be exactly what we want them to be, but who knows better, us or God? He will always provide for us. It may not be in the manner that we think, but He will take care of us.

I went to the cemetery on our third wedding anniversary. I went to Ava's gravesite and laid flowers at her grave. I talked to her and asked her why had she left me alone. I was angry with her and angry at God for allowing this to happen. I started to yell at God and cry out to Him because I couldn't believe that He would allow this to happen and then make me face this situation all alone.

"God, you could have stopped this," I prayed in anger. "I always believed and trusted in you—now I feel so all alone. I need you because the hurt I'm feeling is unbearable. I need your help—I can't handle it alone," I said.

Ava and I had always loved Him and trusted Him. Why had he let us down? Why was He not comforting me? I was so angry that I threw the Bible down and screamed for several minutes.

Finally, I was so distraught that I fell down on my knees and prayed out loud, "God, I can't do this alone. I've been hurting for four months now. I need to know that You're with me. I feel like You've abandoned me. Please show me that You love me. Please give me a sign that You'll always be with me and never forsake me. If I am going to continue in life without Ava, and continue to serve You, I need to know more than ever that You are going to be with me.

"I'm willing to go through life without Ava. But I'm not willing to go through life feeling that You are not with me. I understand that I have to work through the pain, but I need to know You are with me."

All of a sudden—out of nowhere—I felt warm arms wrap around me. I thought that someone in the cemetery had heard me crying and yelling, and had come over and put their arms around me to comfort me. I was hesitant and embarrassed to open my eyes and see who it was, so I squinted one eye open to take a peak at who was hugging me. I looked around and I realized that, physically, there was no one there.

God was saying to me that He was always going to be there, because He loved me. This was a turning point. It marked a change in my heart. I now saw and had actually felt first-hand that God had something special planned for my life. I came away with a new attitude. God had revealed Himself to me that day. I knew God's grace and mercy would sustain me. My life was changed. Changed for the better.

I knew that I would conquer and overcome this tragedy. My faith was a shield—a protector against any thoughts of doubt and despair. Like a knight in battle, I had to carry my faith before me.

The faith that had been established as a young child was coming back to sustain and guide me in this time that I needed it most. Faith had proved to be the cornerstone of my foundation.

CHAPTER 15

FORGIVING THE UNFORGIVABLE

I had only been in the hospital for a short time that fateful night when the word came to me from Mr. and Mrs. Dorsett that the driver who had crashed through our house and killed Ava had been drunk.

I remember thinking that this couldn't be so. I'd done so much with my students to work against this. I had constantly told my students about the danger, irresponsibility, and ignorance a person displays by driving while intoxicated. This couldn't be true. It was too ironic, after all that I'd done to fight against such behavior.

Why was this happening to me? Ava's death was a tragedy, and knowing that a drunk driver had killed her made it worse. I knew more than ever that this tragedy could have been prevented. I was in severe pain; my body felt as if it were on fire. Ava was dead, and I had to hear news like this. Why? Why had this happened? Because of the ignorance, selfishness, and irresponsibility of this one man. This action, which had changed the lives of many, was the result of a poor ten-second decision.

I now found out that he had been drinking for almost the entire day. I was told that he had had problems at work and spent the major part of the day bar hopping. He wasn't just a little intoxicated, he was grossly intoxicated. His blood alcohol content was .19. Estimates were that the driver had the equivalent of fifteen beers in a two-hour period, then got into his truck and tried to drive home. If he had been drinking throughout the day, why didn't someone stop him? If he was with friends, why didn't they stop him? Where were the bartenders? Couldn't they see the condition he was in?

All the feelings of anger and frustration, bitterness and hatred, by this time had reached a boiling point. What would I have done if I got my hands on this guy? Would I wring his neck? The Bible says, "An eye for an eye. A tooth for a tooth," right?

Inside my spirit, something was asking, "Bobby, have you forgotten what you believe? You were brought up in a Christian home and were taught to forgive. Your whole Christian faith is based on forgiveness. That is why Jesus died on the cross. To forgive sinners."

I said to God, "But, God, this man was a drunk driver. He killed my wife. He shouldn't be forgiven. Are you telling me that I have to forgive him?"

I realized now that I was going to have to make a choice. I had to choose to forgive. It wasn't going to happen because of my faith in God. I had to make a conscious choice to forgive. I had to *decide* to do it. This was not going to be easy. It was going to be one of the toughest things I'd ever had to do. As I lay in bed in the hospital with Ava dead only a few hours, I remember praying this prayer.

"Father, I know that I have learned and have been taught since I was a child that I need to forgive those who've wronged me. Christianity is based on forgiveness, and I know the importance of forgiveness to you. God, I know that what I am going to have to deal with and what I'll have to do will be the most difficult thing I have ever had to do in my life. I need Your help and Your strength to do this. I know You want me to forgive this man. But without You, I cannot do this on my own. I now make a choice that I will work at forgiving this man because I also know that if I am going to make it through this tragedy and find healing, I need to forgive."

Now when I say forgive the man, I don't mean that he should walk away scott-free. I think that justice needs to be served. The driver of the pickup was supposed to serve at least eighteen to thirty six months of a ten-year involuntary manslaughter sentence. Too light a sentence, I thought. Sadly, I later found out that he served only four months in jail. He should have served more time. Justice was not carried out. But the point was—I had to forgive.

Forgiving him didn't mean that I was letting him off the hook. It didn't mean it was okay that he had killed Ava, either. It didn't mean that he shouldn't have to pay back something to society. He should have had to pay a price, some kind of price. Breaking the law should cost something.

But I had to forgive him for my sake, so I could be free. Free from hatred. Free from bitterness. Free from the bondage that could enslave me for the rest of my life—unless I released my anger so I could begin to heal. God showed me that He wouldn't be able to fully work in my life until I was willing to fully forgive this man.

Just because I prayed that prayer that night while lying in the hospital bed, and chose to forgive, didn't mean that forgiveness would happen automatically or overnight. Forgiveness is a continual process. It takes a choice. Not an easy one. It's ten seconds at a time. One step at a time. One day at a time. But in the end, it's worth it all. I would not be where I am today if I did not choose to forgive.

With all the pain and loneliness that I was feeling, another straw would have broken the camel's back. This man had already tragically changed my life once in taking Ava from me. If I didn't forgive him, the bitterness would hold me back, and there would be no moving forward in my life. If I didn't work at forgiving this man, he would tragically affect me a second time. First, in taking Ava's life; second, in my not being able to move on with my life and make the best of my situation.

Too many people believe—and they believe this strongly— that by holding a grudge over someone and not forgiving them, they somehow have control, even to the point of putting a "curse" over that person. In this manner they feel that they are getting back at the person. When people hold unforgiveness inside themselves, they are not punishing the other person—they are hurting themselves. The anger and resentment will eat away at them like a slow poison. Slowly. Surely.

Is this the way to live? To repay evil with evil? Think of what kind of world we would have if everyone repaid evil with evil. Unfortunately, with the problems of drugs and guns in many places, this is an alarming reality. Many gangs are instilling hatred and fear in communities, with this principal of evil for evil. That's wrong.

At times I thought I couldn't go on. If I had chosen not to forgive this man, it would have pushed me over the edge. Think what would have happened if I had said, "Okay, buddy. You ruined my life. Now I'm going to ruin yours," then proceeded to hound him or threaten his family, or do some other vengeful thing. In one sense, I had every right to be angry. But if I had taken the law into my own hands and done something foolish to repay this man with evil, I myself would now be in jail, and that would have been a double tragedy.

Ava always used to say to me, "Remember, we are not responsible for how others act toward us or how they treat us, but we are responsible for our actions, reactions, and responses toward them."

Don't let unforgiveness be a roadblock in your life. It can immobilize you, like a flat tire on a car without a spare. If there's a person or persons, or a situation that is keeping you from being the person that God wants you to be, go to that person privately, write them a note, or—if it's too difficult yet to do that—make sure you do your part by forgiving that person. I guarantee that you will feel a huge burden lifted off you. You'll feel as if you can jump to the moon. The chains and bondage that held you hostage will be gone. Now you will be able to move forward with your life and live with freedom.

Let forgiveness be a major part of your life foundation. Choose to forgive today. You can make that choice, but only you can do it. Love is the greatest gift of all. Part of that love is learning how to give and receive forgiveness.

CHAPTER 16

FAMILY AND FRIENDS

Actions speak louder than words. I cannot say it often enough. When a tragedy such as Ava's death happens, you see how important your family and friends are. You also get to see who your true friends are. This becomes clearer by way of how much strength and support you draw from them.

I'll never forget when my mother and sister Debbie walked into my hospital room and saw me all banged up. We all wept uncontrollably. I'll never forget what my mom said to me. She said, "Bobby, I remember when you were a little boy. I could always make the pain go away or help you feel better. But I feel helpless now, because I can't take this pain away from you. If I could, I would. You are going to have to work through this. Just know that I will do all I can to help you."

My sister Debbie wrote about how she felt, seeing me for that first time since the tragedy:

> "When I walked into the hospital room and saw my brother lying in the bed, covered with blood and bandages, I dropped my suitcase and threw myself across him. My mother did the same. We all sobbed together. Racking sobs, straight from the depths of our souls. I knew that I have never felt such anguish and devastation. At that moment I wished that my baby brother had perished along with his beloved wife, so that he would not have to be left here on earth to suffer without her.
>
> "Oh God, I will gladly take his grief upon myself. I can't bear to see him suffer."

Later that same day, Debbie, Mom, and Mrs. D. went to look at my house for the first time since the tragedy. These are words that Debbie used to describe the scene:

> "We walked (me, Mom, Linda Dorsett) into the house at night with a flashlight. I was shocked. It looked like a hurricane had hit this once lovely home. We stumbled over plaster, brick, shattered glass, wood, pieces of furniture, and belongings, dust and debris. The wind whistled and flapped through the heavy black plastic that covered the huge hole that was once the bedroom wall. The feeling was eerie. Doom and despair shivered through my body. I tried hard not to re-create the moment of impact in my mind. I had to get out of there. It was like being in a nightmare or horror movie. Tears sprang from my eyes and I couldn't breathe.
>
> "I'll never forget that sight, and that feeling, the smell—etched in my mind forever."

My mother had left her job and ended up staying with me for the entire three weeks that I was in the hospital. Debbie, who had a four-year-old son, Nicholas, dropped everything to be with me. We've always been a very tight family, and this confirmed to me more than ever how much having a loving and caring family means.

My mother stayed with me by my side for twelve to fourteen hours a day while I was in the hospital and going through my various surgeries. She stayed by my bed from morning 'til night. I had to force her to go back to the Dorsetts' where she was staying. She didn't want to leave me. Knowing that she was with me so many hours each day gave me a comfort that I cannot express.

Debbie was able to be with me for a week and a half before she had to go back to New York. She did all that she could to cheer me up—there were even moments when she made me laugh.

My younger sister, Chrissy, was eighteen at this time. When Ava and I were married, Chrissy had been fifteen and hadn't been sure if she liked Ava too much. Ava was from Texas, Chrissy was very much from New York, and, at that age, Chrissy struggled with my marriage. I was her big brother. Chrissy, like every sister, was only looking out for my best interest.

Twice that summer before the accident, Chrissy had come down to visit Ava and me. It was a great time of growth in the relationship between her and Ava. Chrissy had matured and could now see the type of person Ava was, and that she was a wonderful wife for me. So, when Chrissy heard about the accident, she was especially devastated because she had recently grown to really love Ava after several years of mis-understanding. She called me from New York and told me that she was so hurt she didn't think she would be able to cope with being at the funeral.

My father called me, crying and despondent. It's not often you hear your dad so hurt and in such despair. Though Chrissy and Dad were in New York, I knew their spirits were with me. Throughout my entire recovery period, my family did all they could to support me in every way. Even when I was not so lovable to be around, they tolerated my mood swings. Even when I eventually moved back to New York and said some uncalled for, cruel things, they were under-standing. They were also hurt by the fact that, not only did I lose a wife, but they had lost a daughter-in-law and sister-in-law.

Letters and cards from around the country soon flooded into Friendswood as people heard about the tragedy. I had had no idea how many people loved us until this horrible tragedy occurred. Calls and support from family, friends, and friends of family members came in. I was blown away by the overwhelming response of love and compassion. It not only came from around the country, but around the world. People I didn't know directly were wishing me well and sending their regards. There was a tidal wave of sympa-thy. Hundreds of people called, sent flowers, and donations.

Ava's parents were great. I knew their pain must have been so heavy on their hearts, but they never ceased to show their love for me, even in the loss of their daughter. Mr. D. came to me while I was in the hospital and said to me that he would take care of all the funeral and memorial arrangements. This had to be an unbelievably difficult time for him and Mrs. D. to handle. Ava's parents were with me at the hospital for many hours, and did all they could to comfort me, my family, and my friends. On top of that, they opened their home for me to live with them.

Friends also rallied around me when I needed them most. They really proved what love and friendship was all about. Not only did they come down that weekend, but they also made trips to visit me while I continued to live in Texas, recuperating.

There's an old saying, "You can't pick your family, but you can pick your friends." From the start I knew that I had picked the most awesome friends in the world. Jay Ferraro and his wife, Linda, dropped everything and came. Jakey Jones, who had just graduated from ORU and had taken a new job, told his boss he needed to come down and spend some time with me. Jakey ended up staying a week and a half, and when he returned to Tulsa, his job was no longer there for him. Dave "Riv" Rivera, who had been my resident advisor at ORU and was now working there as an Assistant Dean of Students, came immediately. Joe Liberatore and Chris Harrison, with whom I had played baseball in college, drove the five hundred miles from Tulsa to Friendswood to support me. Joe had just gotten out of the hospital himself, having gone through arthroscopic surgery on his knee that week, and yet he still drove down.

These are the types of friends I had. They would do anything for me. I realized how important my days at ORU had been—the baseball team, former athletes, and others friends showed incredible support for me during this time. Mike Moore, an ex-ORU teammate who was pitching for the Seattle Mariners, gave travel money to Joe and Chris. Cheeks was living in Pittsburgh and, ironically, had just gotten back from touring New York and Connecticut with a theater company where he was performing in plays against drug and alcohol abuse. He left the production without hesitation. I'll never forget Cheeks' face when I first saw him at the house. He had always been a jokester—one who loved to make people laugh and make sure they had a good time—but even Cheeks was very somber. It was the only time I had ever seen him cry. Craig Olson came immediately from Tulsa and was one of the pall bearers.

Rob Kok and his wife Laura came in. So did Toni Swain Fowler and her husband David. The whole Swain family, and especially Toni's younger sister Alli, who was twenty and who would die a year later of cystic fibrosis, came. After I arrived home from the hospital that first day, Alli gave me this little booklet of poems that she had written titled, "Please

Remember… " This meant the world to me because I knew the pain that she was enduring day by day, and the incredible courage that she displayed in fighting her disease. Alli's homemade, handwritten booklet contained these words:

Please Remember… That I Love You

I'd like to capture a rainbow
and stick it in a big box
So that anytime you wanted to,
you could reach in and pull it out.
A piece of sunshine.
I'd like to build you a mountain
that you could call your very own—
A place to find serenity
in those times you feel the need
to be closer to yourself.
I'd like to be the one who's there with you
when you're lonely or troubled
or you just need someone to hold onto…
I'd like to do all this and more
to make your life happy
But sometimes it isn't easy to do the things
I would like to do
Or give the things I would like to give.
So… until I learn how to catch rainbows
and build mountains,
Let me do for you which I know best…
Let me simply be your friend.
You are struggling…
I see it
I feel it
I hurt for you.
But I must tell you, dear friend
I believe with all my heart
that you will emerge somehow wiser,
stronger, and more aware.
Hold onto that thought, tuck it away
in the corner of your heart
Until the hurt melts enough for the learning
To have meaning.
I feel inside of me the sadness of your heart
when things aren't going right.

And my eyes, too, filled with tears—
because I know how you feel,
And because I cherish you so very much
and feel so close by your side.
If only I could
I would right the wrongs and make the days brighter
Because I soon want to see the smile I remember
That sparkles so
When things are going well.
There are times when you have been hurt so badly
That you become certain that the pain will never pass.
But it does...
Sometimes because of your efforts
Sometimes in spite of them,
But always,
Always... it goes away.
So, hold on, and know that tomorrow will come
And with each tomorrow... It will be better.
All I have to offer is my love
to remind you that you're not alone
My hand... to hold and to help
My simple words... that time will take you
to a brighter day,
and strength will walk beside you.
And your heart will show the way.

I read these poems often when I needed to be encouraged. They were a source of strength from one so young and so fragile herself. Allison Swain died of cystic fibrosis in 1986. I know that I will see her someday. I can't wait to tell her how much she meant to me.

The pastors, staff, and congregation from Lakewood Church and Friendswood United Methodist Church were always present to help, too.

Gary Causey, a friend of mine and vice principal at Santa Fe High School, was at the hospital regularly. He shared with me how my experience was drawing him closer to God. He had a family and other responsibilities, but somehow he made it a priority to be with me. He came to my bedside one night in the hospital, crying, and said, "Remember the night of the accident, when you and I were talking at the football game in Wharton—we were talking about God and you said that sometimes people make ignorant and irresponsible choices and that they can't blame God? That really hit home to me when this happened to you—and I found out this guy was a drunk driver."

The Ragland Family—Joe, Linda, Shelly, and Joey, had me over to their house for dinner once or twice a week. They took me out with them. We saw the Harlem Globetrotters together. They even took me on a family trip to Colorado to see the Rocky Mountains. They made me feel welcome, loved, and part of their family. They'll never realize in a million years the impact that their compassion had on me. It's exactly what I needed. The Raglands were sent. I know they were.

The other person who was absolutely awesome was my friend Saleim. Sometimes he would come by himself and sometimes he would bring his girlfriend, but for three weeks straight Saleim was there with me at the hospital. He always stayed late into the night, mostly past midnight and into the wee hours of the morning. He would stay so my mother and Mrs. Dorsett could go home and get some rest.

During the whole time immediately after the accident and in the time that I stayed in Texas as I recovered, I saw how vital my family and friends were to me. One of the reasons that I was able to come through this ordeal as well as I did was because of their constant love and support.

Ava wrote something about friendship that I have saved all these years:

> "A friend is one with whom you dare to be yourself. And as we share ourselves, we also learn more about ourselves. A friend is someone with whom you can truly share all the important aspects and dimensions of your heart that make you—you. Who makes being excited about something so much more delicious as they delight in the pleasure you are experiencing. Someone you can be quiet and mellow with, when you don't feel like talking, but just basking in His presence and tasting His riches. Even though the rest of your world expects you to have it all together— to have all the answers—a friend allows you to be confused, and ask questions, knowing as you seek truth you will find it, and be that much richer in real knowledge. A friend is someone

whom you always feel loved by, and know that
in your weakness, you are accepted."

She concluded on the back of that piece of college-ruled
plain notebook paper:

"Live life to the fullest. Get the most from
each hour, each day of your life. Then you can
look forward with confidence; and back without
regrets."

I knew that it would take every ounce of strength that I
had to make it through this time of grief. My youth had
taught me the importance of strong relationships. My friends
and family had come in the time of need. The people who
needed to be there *were* there and could be counted on. I
wouldn't trade them for anything in the world. I have been
blessed with the third solid brick in my foundation—family
and friends. If you were there for me in any way at all,
thank you, thank you, thank you.

CHAPTER 17

FIGHT

There once was a woman with an "issue of blood"; that is, she had a blood-borne disease and had to live with other sick people who were not allowed to come into towns or anyplace close to other inhabitants. Period.

As the Bible story goes, she followed Jesus and touched the hem of his garment. As soon as she did this, Jesus said, "Who touched my garment?" The woman finally came forth and said, "I did." "Your faith has made you whole," said Jesus. This is an encouraging story to me because, first of all, this was a woman, not a man. And women in those days and in that society were not treated as equals of men. They were considered second-class citizens. Second, she was considered "unclean." And third, it was forbidden to touch a holy person. Yet, she was willing to fight for what she loved so dearly—life itself. She fought for her life by touching the holy one, Jesus.

When you think about people who have truly overcome adversity and conquered major obstacles in life, you realize they did it by depending on the strength of their own foundation—one that had already been established. Triumphant people seem to have foundational principles in common. Whether we talk about overcomers like Dennis Byrd, Robert Schuller, Andre Thornton, Dave Roever, W Mitchell, Terry Law, or Skip Wilkins, certain similarities exist. Their foundations stood firm through the turbulent storms they had to weather. And some have had to weather hurricanes.

Common denominators of triumphant people are determination, drive, and a fighting spirit. Many have also relied on faith, family, friends, the willingness to forgive, and love to help them through their difficulties. Their determination is so strong that they will not allow their problems to destroy them. The will, the guts, the motivation to conquer the challenge are all present. There is a desire in a triumphant person to meet the challenge head-on and not be intimidated by the confrontation.

This is true in sports as in life. So much of sports is more psychological than physical. Why does the coach give a pep talk to his team right before they take the field for a game? He knows that on any given day, one team can beat another. His athletes may not be as physically talented as their opponents that day, but if they can believe they can win, play as a team, execute the plays better than the other team—then they have a better chance to win. Every year in sports there are always upsets in which a David slays a Goliath. You can probably name two or three occasions when that has happened. That's what makes life so exciting—you must prepare to win.

The next time you are watching a basketball game on television, if one team suddenly makes a run of eight or ten consecutive points, look at the faces of both teams. One will undoubtedly have the look of defeat or despair, the other will be jubilant and pumped with enthusiasm and elation. This is the psychological factor that can make or break a game. The coach of the losing team, if he's a good coach, will either call a time out or find a way to instill confidence in his team so that they never give up. It's all about the will, the guts, the motivation. Never, ever give up.

To achieve victory, each of us has to take advantage of one of the greatest gifts of all—freedom of choice. Victory doesn't just happen within a person's life. Careers don't just happen overnight. Movie stars and athletes may seem to appear "overnight," but don't kid yourself. You can be sure that those people put in countless, unseen hours of hard work and sweat to get where they are. Their work was unknown and unnoticed possibly for years, but they still did it. They chose to do it. They paid their dues to get to the top.

Remember that and ask yourself, Are you willing to pay the price for what you want to achieve? Are you willing to make that choice? Are you willing to sacrifice? We must all count the cost. Anything that is worthwhile in life takes time, sweat, and determination.

In my situation I knew that I would have to continually battle to put my life back together. I also knew that I would have to fight through these things all the way until I reached a point of final decision and had triumphed and overcome them so that I could get on with my life.

Since I was a child, I've always had a fierce competitive nature. This same fierce *will to win* and *never give up* now helped me in my struggle against despair and anguish over the loss of so much in my life.

I had a basis for the faith in myself to never give up. My freshman year in high school I had fought to make the junior varsity baseball team. Here I was, Rico Petrocelli's nephew, supposed to be a great player because of my uncle's reputation, not mine, and I was fighting to make the team. The first half of the season I ended up not starting, but I worked hard to prove myself and ended up starting the second half of the season.

The highlight of the year was when I hit a grand slam against one of the top teams in our district. I finished up strong and ended up as one of the best players on the team. The main point here was that I never gave up. I remembered that, even if you start slowly, you can finish strong—and that will make a difference.

My sophomore year in high school, the J.V. baseball program was cut for budget reasons. I tried out for the varsity, but partly due to an injury, I didn't make the team. I said to myself that I was going to work harder and make the team as a junior. That summer I worked harder and harder, and made the varsity team. In both my junior and senior years I started in centerfield and made a name for myself in baseball.

When I attended ORU, I tried out for the team my first two years there. After not making the varsity either time, I vowed over the summer between my sophomore and junior years that I would work harder than ever and come back and make the team. That summer I lifted weights, I ran, I took batting practice, and worked hard. I was ready for tryouts that fall. After the first day of tryouts, the coach came up to me and said, "I can't believe how much you've improved." I was determined. I worked hard to develop the skills that God gave me. My reward was that I ended up making the team both my junior and senior years at ORU.

Fear had invaded my heart and was trying to destroy me in any way it could. Anytime I went to sleep, in the back of my mind I wasn't sure that I wouldn't once again wake up in the same nightmare situation. Day in and day out I had to fight the battle against fear constantly. I wondered if I would ever have a full life again. If I would ever teach again. If I would ever love again. If people would laugh or accept the way I looked.

Could I go to sleep at night in peace and not fear someone else crashing into my house? That may seem crazy to have a fear of that, but can you imagine anyone ever believing that such a thing could happen in the first place?

Fear can cloud your mind and your heart so that you can't enjoy things fully. After a traumatic event, it's always lurking in the back of your mind.

Another battle I had to fight against was guilt. How could I enjoy life again? Ava was dead. How could I ever laugh again? Ava was dead. How could I ever look for love again? Ava was my love. I felt that I was now turning my back on her. Why didn't I lift the truck off of her? Why didn't I dig her out? Why didn't I get to her? If she was my wife, why didn't I protect her?

I felt guilty that just two months before the accident we had switched the sides of the bed that we slept on. What if we had not switched and I had been on the other side? Maybe I could've withstood the impact. We had also talked about sleeping in a different bedroom. What if we had slept in another room? Maybe she wouldn't be dead. What if we had rented one of the other houses farther back? What if I had taken that job up in New Jersey? We wouldn't have been in Texas at all. I had to live with the guilt of all of these questions. What if... What if... What if...? They kept coming back.

I felt guilty that I wasn't the one who had been killed. Why was she taken and I wasn't?

While I lived with Ava's family following the accident, I sometimes wondered what they were thinking. Did they ask, Why did Ava have to die? Why wasn't it Bobby? I don't know if they ever thought that, but I couldn't help but realize how difficult it must have been for them.

Even in the hospital immediately following the accident—it had only been hours since Ava's death—I sat there on the gurney in the hallway and wondered if Ava's family wished it had been me who had been killed instead of her.

Something that made me feel good was a visit from Ava's Uncle Ted. Ted came one day to visit me in the hospital and said, "Bobby, I want you to know that we're glad you're alive."

He'll never know what that meant to me. He seemed to be saying, "We're not happy that Ava was killed, but we are happy that *you're* alive. We love you—because you're family, too."

Life is filled with battles. We all fight against fear, guilt, confusion, bitterness, hatred, even unforgiveness. But we must press on and not allow obstacles to hinder our progress. A true champion may lose a battle, but the fight in him is so fierce that he picks himself up—to fight on and win the war.

CHAPTER 18

FEEDING GOOD THINGS

The last foundation principle is feeding. When we think about "feeding," we automatically think about food. Or at least I do. Well, I had to not only feed my body, but also other areas of my life that needed special nourishment. I had to choose to feed my mind, my body, and my spirit good things. "You are what you eat." It's true. And this applies to all areas of your life—not just the physical part.

While attending Oral Roberts University, the importance of feeding and uplifting every part of your life, "the whole man," was heavily emphasized. Learning to live a balanced life was one thing that was always stressed. Spirit, Body, and Mind. I knew that it was tremendously important that I have all three of these areas in some sort of balance if I were to overcome what had happened to me.

I believe that there are two kinds of music, positive and negative. Positive music feeds your mind good, healthy, and wholesome things. Negative music can tear down your spirit and have a detrimental effect on you as a person. I had to make sure that I was listening to positive music. Music is such a huge part of my life. I listen to music when I wake up in the morning. I listen to music on the drive to work every day. Sometimes at work, I may be able to softly play some background music. It was imperative that I listen to music that would build me up and not tear me down.

I'm a big fan of praise and worship music. This is positive music, music that renews and refreshes your mind and spirit. It's uplifting and has the power of restoration. I believe there is power in praise. I listened to praise music to help lift my spirit when I felt despair. Happy, upbeat music put me in a good frame of mind.

There's a song I remember as a child that said, "In my heart there rings a melody. Rings a melody. Rings a melody.

In my heart there rings a melody—there rings a melody of love." I learned this in church during Sunday school class in Brooklyn at the age of eight. Who would've guessed that such a simple child's tune would be such a comfort years later?

Sometimes I listened to speakers or preachers who had positive messages of hope and life. People like Tom Landry, former coach of the Dallas Cowboys; John Wooden, the legendary basketball coach of UCLA; Norman Vincent Peale, author of *The Power of Positive Thinking*; Robert Schuller, from the Crystal Cathedral in California; Oral Roberts, who always said, "God is my source"; Don Shula, the inspirational head coach of the Miami Dolphins, was also one of my favorite speakers because of his drive to win and his constant pursuit of excellence.

This daily regimen of feeding my mind positive things encouraged me to persevere and press on, and to never ever give up. I had a steady "diet" of uplifting music and positive speakers to consume. Sometimes I needed an appetizer, other times a soup or salad and, occasionally, a full-course dinner, depending on how I felt at that moment.

But the best thing about feeding on positive morsels like this was that I could never be guilty of overeating. I could "eat" to my heart's content. I needed the nourishment and realized that I had to constantly renew my mind, my body, and my spirit. The psychological trauma had wounded my spirit so deeply that I needed to rejuvenate it with good things.

In addition to getting my mind back in good shape, I also began to get back into shape physically. I began to train on weights again, lifting every other day, doing lat pulls, bent-over rows, tricep extensions, squats, and bench presses.

I also began light jogging and jogging in the pool to increase my endurance and aerobic capacity. I was expending more energy during the day and therefore had to refuel more often. I had to make sure that I fed my body good food—like fruits, vegetables, and other healthy items—and not junk foods that would stunt my growth and hinder my progress. Being from a physical education background, I knew that exercise and diet go hand in hand when it comes to athletic performance. Since I realized I could've easily been more seriously injured, I was excited that I could still work out, play basketball, and exercise.

As I physically got stronger and back into shape, I also felt much more confident about my appearance. For the longest time, I had reservations about going to the beach—one of my favorite places in all the world. But because of the scars and blemishes that will never go away, I had to accept the fact that every time I wore shorts and a short-sleeve shirt, people knowingly and unknowingly would stare at me. I had to get used to small children pointing and cringing at the sight of the deep, massive scars on my legs and arms.

"Mommy, mommy. Look at that man's arm!" a little girl would innocently yell so that the whole beach could hear.

"Honey, it's not polite to... Oh, my gosh—George. George. What do you think happened to that man over there? Jessica, stop pointing."

Believe me, I've heard it all. Sometimes, if someone asked me what happened, I'd be tempted to say with a straight face, "Oh, I was swimming in three or four feet of water right out there and a great white shark bit me about this same time last year. A lot of people think they're deadly, but I survived okay, see?"

I never did, though. That would've been really mean. I just took a deep breath, gained my composure, and explained to them the story. Most of them were apologetic and receptive after that.

Spiritually, I prayed, attended church, listened to praise music, read the Bible, and referred to other self-help inspirational books. Mentally, my mind was being renewed by meditating and thinking upon good things: Wholesome music, inspirational leaders, uplifting poems, positive writings, and motivating speakers. Physically, I balanced my diet with exercise. Focusing on all three areas was the only way for me to gain a total victory and get my life back together.

Another way that I was able to cope with the grief from the tragedy was to fill my heart with laughter—joyous, hearty laughter. "A merry heart doeth good like a medicine" (Proverbs 17:22). Since I am a huge fan of many of the classic television comedies, one of my favorite escapes was to watch various episodes of my favorites. This was wonderful therapy for me because if I were feeling sad or depressed, I could pop in some tapes and sit there for hours and laugh hysterically at the antics on the screen.

One of my favorite "Three Stooges" episodes is when Curly dressed up like a gorilla. One of my favorite "Lucy" shows is "Vitameatavegamin," where she was the spokeswoman for a new health supplement. A favorite "Honeymooners" episode is when Norton was teaching Ralph to dance. The chemistry between Art Carney and Jackie Gleason on that show helped to make it one of the best of all time. And one of the most memorable "Little Rascals" short films is the one in which Alfalfa fights for Darla's affection by building a boat to race Waldo, the rich snobby kid. I love that particular one because it has Spanky, Buckwheat, and Porky in it also.

After all these years, I have an extensive collection of these nostalgic and classic comedies. Every once in a while, when I need a good strong, belly laugh, I'll pop in a tape and away I'll go.

There's a lot of truth to the statement, "Garbage in—Garbage out." I like to say, "Positive in—Positive out."

Remember that the sum total of what you are as a person is only as good as the sum total of the parts that you put in.

CHAPTER 19

CAN I LOVE AGAIN?

When school ended in the spring of 1986, I knew that Texas was not where I wanted to stay. I needed to return to New York to find myself again, and to determine in which direction I wanted to go with my life. I thought I would feel more comfortable in familiar surroundings. So back to New York I went. I didn't know what was ahead for me—but I felt a peace about taking the step.

Mineola High School on Long Island hired me as a full-time substitute teacher and junior varsity and varsity football coach for the first two months of the fall semester. Though I had just spent three years as a full-time teacher and coach in Texas, I knew that here I was starting over. I also knew this was the first step to securing a full-time teaching position.

Fortunately, I didn't have to wait long. In the short time that I was in Mineola, I gained a lot of favor with the faculty, students, and staff. I also found a new strength in myself that would eventually point me in the direction of becoming a full-time motivational speaker.

Mineola High School has one of the best Students Against Driving Drunk programs in the country. The sponsor and student leaders of the group asked me to share my story in their major fall assembly program. Representatives from *Reader's Digest* magazine, politicians, and many successful community leaders were to be in attendance.

The audience was predicted to be around one thousand people. The date of the assembly would be October 25, 1986, exactly one year to the day after the accident. I was nervous to be speaking so soon after the accident.

For weeks prior to the program, I wrote down ideas and prepared for what I would speak about that day. I not only wanted to give a good speech, but I also wanted to communicate as sincerely as possible that no one should *ever* have to go through what I had gone through. The loss was too great, and the pain was too deep.

But most of all I wanted to strongly and effectively relay the message that had to be driven home—that this type of tragedy *could have* been and *can* be prevented in the future. I didn't sleep well the night before the program. I was too excited and nervous, hoping that it would go well and that the response would be positive.

"The reason that I'm standing before you today... " I had practiced my speech a hundred times before actually standing in front of this audience, going over and over the key points, and stressing different parts of it to get the proper emphasis. I was so pumped up, I bet everybody thought I was going to explode. You see, I'm the type of person who tells it like it is—what you see is what you get. I would never be good in poker because I wear my heart on my sleeve and my emotions show in my face too easily. I'm a straightforward kind of guy, and I don't beat around the bush. Maybe that's my strongest point in speaking—that I come across as genuine and sincere. Maybe because I am. I want so badly to communicate effectively that I just bluntly tell the truth.

The day of the speech was a landmark day for me, the beginning of a new era in my life. After the first few moments of my speech, something kicked in. I think it was the fact that I was just telling my story, with no sugarcoating whatsoever. The truth and reality came through to the audience that day, and their response was exhilarating. I knew in my heart that from my speaking for the very first time in that assembly program at Mineola High School on October 25, 1986, seeds were planted for my future in speaking and helping young people with my message. This was the first time that I began to see that somehow God was going to bring good out of something that was terrible—a miracle that only He could do.

Since things had gone so well in my short time at Mineola High School, by November I was offered a full-time teaching position in the East Norwich-Oyster Bay school district. I was now teaching physical education and was a high school assistant coach in football, baseball, and basketball. This was only the beginning of more good things to come. I was happy to be back in New York. Long Island is a lot different than the Brooklyn area, but, hey, it's New York. I felt a peace about the move from Texas, and landing the teaching position after only a few months was confirmation that I had made the right choice.

It was now a year and a half since the accident and I was starting to feel better about myself in more areas of my life. I was teaching and coaching in a new environment. I was spending time with the kids, whom I loved, and I was in familiar and comfortable surroundings.

The next thing that I wanted to get back was a feeling of companionship. I was open to a relationship, but decided that I would not actively seek one out. A lot of people were giving me different advice about that area of my life. One would say, "Go to this club and find a nice girl. There's tons of beautiful girls there. So-and-so met a girl there, and they've been going out for three months now. Who knows? They might even get married. They're talking about living together first. You ever thought about trying that for awhile?"

Someone else would say, "Bobby, come on. You're young. Just go out and pick one. There are all kinds of fish in the sea. Just throw out your hook and reel one in." Another would say, "I've got a friend who has a sister in her mid-twenties. She doesn't go out much, but she's a very nice girl. She's smart, intelligent, has a lot of brains—a really sharp girl. Did I mention that she's very nice? Her mother keeps telling her, 'Live a little. Take off three of those sweaters, shave, and go out on a date like a good girl...'"

Everybody tried to give me advice about love. I was beginning to think that maybe I was ready for a relationship, but I wanted it to come naturally.

Soon I met a beautiful young woman by the name of Suzanne Marie Nick. She was from Long Island, and she was absolutely gorgeous. She was from a strong family with a traditional Catholic background. Her ethnic heritage was Polish and German.

I remember the first time I laid eyes on her. A coaching friend had introduced her to me while we were getting pizza at a small pizzeria on Long Island. When I said "Hi" to her, my heart almost leaped out of my throat. "My name is Bobby Petrocelli... It's nice to meet you," I said as my jaw dropped to the floor. She was a Babe—with a capital B.

Babe-a-lonia. Babe-a-licious. Babe-raham Lincoln. She could've said, "Four score and seven years ago..." and I would've hung on every word. I think she felt the same about me, because when our eyes met, we both experienced a deep, fixating gaze, as if we were both spellbound and entranced with each other. I'll never forget that feeling. It was a moment of unmistakable connection, like two puzzle pieces finding their matching groove. The fit was there. We knew something exciting would be happening for as long as we wanted it to. But the best part about it was that we knew from that first moment there was something special between us.

Everybody called her Suzy. I liked that. Even her name had a ring to it. Suzy Nick. I've been told that one of the major differences between men and women is that men are much more stimulated by sight, and women are more stimulated by how they're treated. Well, whatever the case, Suzy had caught my eye. She was a knockout. She had long, athletic legs with well-defined calves. She had the face of a beautiful fashion model. Her hair was long and dark, the kind she could fix in a million different ways so the style would always look fresh and new. Her personality was full of energy, full of life, and a lot of fun to be with. She had everything that I liked in a woman—in abundance, I might add. She was a 15+ on a scale of 1 to 10. And, to top it off, she was an athlete, a volleyball and basketball player.

Without question, she had an *invisible touch*. I remember that first time I met Suzy. She looked at me in such a way. *Wow!* I said to myself. There was a gleam in her eyes, and my eyes were gleaming, too, and my smile was beaming.

Suzy was young and full of life. She caused my heart to skip a beat. Before this time I had felt a void, a place that only a special woman could fill. Now I hoped and prayed Suzy would be that special woman. Something was definitely there—something magical between us.

Some people look for this kind of magic all of their lives. I was ecstatic to think that I'd found it—again. For a second blessed time.

As Suzy and I grew closer in our relationship, I was still

haunted by doubts that I could ever really love again. Could I? I wasn't sure. I did know that she brought much joy into my life when I was with her, the kind of joy that I had longed for. A joy that I had known God would restore.

With every girlfriend in my life, I've always looked for the chemistry between us. There's a lot to be said about how you feel when you're around a person. Does she make you feel comfortable? Are you able to be yourself in any situation? Does she make you a better person? Are you making her a better person? This is what I call chemistry. There's got to be that special kind of bonding, like two halves fitting together to make a whole.

I felt this with Suzy. We liked a lot of the same things. She liked different ethnic foods. She liked Italian dishes. Our first date was at an Italian restaurant in Brooklyn named Callaro's. I can still remember what Suzy ordered: chicken parmesan—great! It is one of my favorite dishes, also. I remember how nervous we both were as we ate our food, wanting to make the proper impression.

At first, Suzy wasn't thrilled with another favorite food of mine—Mexican. But after I introduced her to Chi Chi's and authentic Mexican food, she quickly became accustomed to it, and today Mexican is one of her favorite foods. She now craves Mexican foods—Hallelujah!

She loved sports and also loved to *watch* sports with me. She didn't mind watching college football or basketball with me, which are two of my favorite sports to watch. I love college sports. Maybe even more than the pros.

We even shared the same idiosyncrasies. I'm an ex-baseball player and she's an ex-softball player, and occasionally we talked about our habits while playing.

"You're probably going to think this is weird..." I started to say, then changed my mind. "Well... never mind."

"You can't start a statement like that and not finish it," she scolded me.

"Well, it's kind of a stupid thing and you probably won't understand. When I play sports..."

"...you can't chew gum and play at the same time," she interjected before I could finish.

"That's right. How'd you know that?" I asked.

"You can't do it because it ruins your concentration," she continued.

"Right. I can't. Who told you that?"

"I just knew," Suzy said. "I can't chew gum and play sports at the same time, either. It ruins my concentration."

I couldn't believe it. This to me was a major connection. How did she know I felt that way? And how in the world did I meet somebody I liked so well and who, on top of everything, had exactly the same weird problem in playing sports. To me, this was nothing short of miraculous. It *had* to be God who had brought us together. Things just don't happen this way.

I quickly realized that *this* woman was special. We really clicked. Certain things truly impressed me about Suzy. I was eight years older than her, but she had a great maturity about her. Could I really be falling madly in love with a younger woman?

I was impressed and touched by her interest in me as a person. She asked questions about my life—my relationship with Ava, and talked about how hard it must have been to work through the tragedy. She seemed to have a genuine love, concern, and compassion for me. She was genuinely interested in what made me tick. She expressed herself in such a way that it made me feel whole again. Comfortable again. Attractive again. When I looked at Suzy I could see that she had strong feelings towards me, too. I could see it simply and truthfully in her eyes—she really loved me. I knew it was more than a physical thing, because just to be with her was special in itself.

I knew that love had bitten me again. And once again it left deep tooth marks.

The first gift Suzy ever gave me was at the beach. We were on our second date when she handed me a gift-wrapped box.

"I have something for you, Bobby," she said as we sat on the edge of the pier. I took the box and felt that it had definite weight to it.

I smiled at her, not knowing what to say because she had caught me off guard and taken me by surprise. But I loved every minute of it. I slowly peeled away the gift wrapping and opened the box. My eyes lit up as I saw what the contents were—a spray bottle of Obsession cologne. Was she trying to tell me something? Whatever it was, I didn't care. All I know is the next time she saw me I was wearing

Obsession. If Suzy gave it to me because it was her favorite, I would wear it every minute of every day.

Looking back at it now, that's one of the reasons that I liked to be with her. It was because she often surprised me with things like this. She was often unpredictable; so full of life, energy, and unpredictability. But the best thing was, she enjoyed being that way just for me.

The more time I spent with her, the more I fell in love with Suzy. We would talk for hours, whether at the beach, on the phone, or just sitting around the house. I felt so comfortable with her—she was so very easy to open up to. I liked that she asked questions and really wanted to know the answers. I liked that she wasn't the type of woman who only wanted to talk about herself and her own problems. I liked that she wasn't the type of woman to take and not give back.

She never seemed to be threatened that I had been married before. She accepted it as part of my life. She realized that she couldn't change the past, but could maybe become part of my future. She loved me for who I was. I began to ask myself, "Could I love twice? Could I be so privileged to meet such an incredible woman?" My hopes ran high. Why shouldn't they? We had so much in common and had hit it off so well. There had to be a future for us somewhere. This relationship was feeling too comfortable and too complete for it not to lead to more.

I just knew something extra special was there.

One night at my mother's house in Brooklyn, I knew Suzy had to pass the biggest test of all. I popped in a "Three Stooges" video to see her response. If she laughed, then she wasn't the girl for me. But if she laughed *hysterically*—I was on the right track.

Suzy fell on the floor laughing so hard it brought tears to her eyes. My eyes also began to tear, not necessarily because of the stooges antics, but because I now realized that love had truly found me again.

Perhaps the icing on the cake was that Suzy had a great desire to know more about God. This, to me, was encouraging and important. I saw the depth that she had in her life, and it electrified me. She understood the importance of the greater things in life.

One evening when I went back home after dropping Suzy at her place, I sat in my house and wondered if this was really happening. *Please let this love be real*, I said to God. For the longest time I had thought that there was some sort of curse on me that would keep me from ever being in love again. Isn't that something? What a lie. What an outright lie! But the sad thing is there are people today who are feeling this way. They think that there is some kind of curse that is keeping them from some type of happiness. There is not. Let me say it again—*there is not*. That's a lie, a lie that has to be dealt with. But still I was afraid that if I invested my love in Suzy that maybe, just maybe, the same thing would happen, and she too would be taken from me. Can you see the kind of fear that I was living under? When bad things happen to us, many times we tend to shut down. We withdraw out of fear. We have to choose not to do this.

On what would have been my fourth wedding anniversary if Ava were still alive—March 12, 1987—I was at Suzy's house when she handed me several boxes of presents. I didn't know why I was being blessed this way.

"You know why!" she exclaimed.

I pondered, confused.

"You know what day this is, don't you?" she asked.

Then it dawned on me. She was so concerned about what type of negative emotions I might have that day that she wanted to do something positive for me to cheer me up. I knew more than ever that I wanted a serious relationship with her. My involvement with Suzy was now allowing me to put my past in the proper perspective. Suzy knew how much I enjoyed writing my thoughts and feelings down in a journal and had bought one for me. In March 1987 I wrote this down after she gave it to me:

> "My life has been through so much. I thank you, Lord, for always seeing me through. You have always been there for me. You have now given me the chance to love again. Such a wonderful, loving, and understanding young lady to share my life with. The last several months have only been the beginning of many more wonder-

ful months and years in our relationship. Let us always keep our hearts and eyes focused on you.

"It's through your loving hand that we can experience the love we have for each other. Help us to encourage, build up, and not tear down one another. Jesus, let your peace and love guide us through all the journeys of our lives together. Give me the strength to overcome fear, doubt, and insecurity. Let your confidence rule in my life, for you are my confidence and strength.

"Thank you again for Suzy, your precious gift to me. Let me be precious to her always. Guide us to lead others to your saving and loving Grace. Help us to be strong in you. To please you, our God, in all we do."

"Hey, why don't we ride to the beach today?" I nonchalantly asked Suzy on June 2, 1988, when I met her after work. "We can go to Angelo's Pizza and get a bite to eat. How's that sound?" I had just come from Donato's Jewelry Store in the heart of the "Diamond Exchange" in Manhattan.

"Fine," Suzy said, unwittingly.

It was a sunny day and we arrived at the Jones Beach West End-2 at 4:30. The beach was virtually empty, so we walked and talked and casually strolled around the sand. A couple of times I thought the timing was right, but I didn't do it. Then, about five o'clock, after we had been talking for a while, I dropped to both knees.

"Suzy, what are you doing for the next fifty years?" I asked. "I was wondering if you wouldn't mind marrying me very much?"

She waved her arms in the air like a chicken trying desperately to fly and started screaming, "Yes! Yes! Yes! I will! I will! I *will* marry you!"

She cried, laughed, and jumped around like a jumping bean. The seagulls ran for cover and the ocean did "the wave." When she said "Yes," it brought such joy to my heart. All those times of doubt and despair had been shattered. God had blessed me with two diamonds. A 1.12 carat marquise ring from Donato's and, more importantly, a precious diamond of a woman—in Suzanne Marie Nick.

We saved two special shells from the beach that day, to remind us of that wonderful day when Suzy said "Yes" and jumped around like a jumping bean.

On May 6, 1989, Suzy and I were married in a beautiful garden ceremony at Westbury Manor in Westbury, New York. To give you another example of God's blessings on me, rain had fallen for several straight days before the ceremony, and we were disappointed early that Saturday morning because it looked as if we would have to hold the wedding indoors. But wouldn't you know, about forty-five minutes before the ceremony, the skies cleared and we were able to be married outside. It had rained for days and days and days, and this was the first time it had cleared up. Is God faithful? I know that He was smiling a big smile on that day.

It was awesome to have the family and friends who had supported me through my trials and the tragedy now be part of this victorious celebration. I think they were almost as happy for me as I was. I said *almost*. The wedding was such a joy-filled celebration. Everything about it was special. You could feel it.

The reception dinner was terrific, also. Since Suzy had never been married before and we were starting our life together, I tried to make it as special as possible. I sang to her a ballad called, "I've Waited a Lifetime." Right after my best man Jay Ferraro proposed a toast, I asked for the microphone, sat Suzy in the middle of the room in a chair, and started to sing with an accompaniment tape.

> *"I've waited a lifetime*
> *To stand here looking in your eyes.*
> *Now it's finally coming true.*
> *With the Lord as my witness,*
> *I'll love you for the rest of my days,*
> *Don't you ever go away.*
> *Nobody else*
> *Can make me smile the way you do.*
> *Nobody else*
> *Can ever win my heart like you... "*

Suzy cried, and I saw everyone in the place crying—

family, friends, guests, waiters, waitresses, the maitre d'—
even the band. It was an emotional and special time for not
only me, but for everyone who loved both Suzy and me.
There was barely a dry eye in the house. Cheeks told me it
was because my voice was so terrible. He said I broke two
mirrors, three priceless crystal sculptures, and Mrs. O'Leary's
glasses. You see the kind of friends I have? You see the kind
of abuse I take?

I know they were crying because they realized all that I
had gone through. This was the day I got a second chance
at love. My family and friends knew the pain and devastation I had been through, and now to see me with such joy
in my heart filled their eyes with tears. Person after person
came up to us after the ceremony and said that it was one
of the best times that they had ever had at a wedding.
There was such an overwhelming sense of celebration and
sheer joy, that it enveloped the room with its warmth and
blanketed us all with a true feeling of happiness. I was starting over, but it was a new beginning for my princess, my
beautiful baby, Suzy.

Following the celebration and reception, Suzy and I spent
our wedding night at the La Guardia Airport Marriott. I
spent a major part of the evening crying tears of joy.

We walked into the room and nearly fell over with exhaustion. That's when it hit us. I think it hit me first, and
then Suzy's reaction to my tearful release was to also cry. It
felt so cleansing to get it out. All my emotion from the past
several years was released when I allowed myself to weep
tears of joy. My life had almost been destroyed, but was
now looking full of hope and promise. That to me was
nothing short of a miracle. We were both so thankful to
God for bringing us together.

Suzy and I honeymooned in the Outer Banks of North
Carolina. We were planning a longer honeymoon cruise
later that summer because I couldn't afford much time off
from work in May.

We had moved to Virginia in August 1988 and I was teaching physical education and coaching football at Great Bridge
High School in Chesapeake. Suzy was a student at Old Dominion University in Norfolk, completing her degree.

Following our honeymoon, we returned to Chesapeake

where we had purchased a new home. The cost of living in Virginia was much less than in New York, and we were able to have a beautiful, traditional brick home built for much less than in New York. Our new home had hardwood floors, a fireplace, cherry furniture, four bedrooms, lots of space, and a beautiful yard, and was in a new development.

I stood in the bedroom of our new home and said to Suzy, "The last four years I've felt like a nomad. A wanderer. A man who couldn't call any place 'home.' Now that we're married and together, I want you to know that I feel I *am* home again." I tried to hold it back, but the emotion was too strong to suppress any longer. I felt a freedom in my heart as I began to cry—the joy of starting our lives together had overwhelmed me. I couldn't keep it inside.

Suzy held me as I cried for several minutes. "I love you, Bobby Petrocelli. There's nothing in this world that can keep you from my love. Always remember that," she sweetly whispered in my ear as she embraced me tighter. I hugged her back, but there was no way I could've gotten close enough to her at that moment. We had become one. And I had become whole. Again.

Suzy and I have been able to live life to the fullest. We've traveled, been on cruises, shared times at the beach. She's my friend. I need that in my wife. She's my best, best friend. I love doing things with my best friend. I love for her to experience the best in life.

"No man can possibly know what life means, what the world means, until he has a child and loves it. And then the whole universe changes and nothing will ever again seem exactly as it seemed before." —Lafcadio Hearn

One fear that kept creeping up and showing its ugly face through those years after the tragedy was that I wasn't sure I could father children. When the truck ran over me, my testicles were injured, and they swelled up to the size of a tennis ball. I was too embarrassed about it to have a doctor check to see if I was sterile, but in the back of my mind I constantly wondered if I would ever have children. I love kids and wanted the chance to have a family and be a father. I didn't know if I could.

On April 11, 1992, at 3:30 p.m., that fear was put to rest when Alec Robert Petrocelli was born. My first child. My first son. It was a miracle. I never thought that such a little red person could bring me such joy.

Cheeks called him the "Red Man of Courage." Alec Robert. If it were up to Suzy, his name would have been Alec Tom Cruise Petrocelli. You see what type of wife I have? My first child was eight pounds, twelve ounces, and twenty-one inches long, a future defensive lineman. The Giants need him bad. He is adorable. So beautiful and handsome. And he looks just like his daddy.

Rarely do I call him Alec. I call him Pookey Hahny. What silly names we call our children. "What's up, Champ? What are you looking at, Pookey Hahny? Are you looking at Daddy?" I say to him in his crib. It's silly, isn't it, the way we talk to babies? Probably because they bring us so much happiness. And we can't believe that a human life started from a little seed. How can people say there are no miracles happening today? How can people say, "There is no God?" Every time a child is born it's a miracle. Both a miracle *and* a beautiful gift from God.

Suzy spent six hours in labor after her water broke. Alec had a large head and it took more time to push him out than normal. He got stuck twice, once in the cervix and once in the birth canal. Finally, a vacuum extractor was brought in to help bring Alec into the world. Suzy was a tough cookie. She had Alec by natural childbirth. No epidural. No sedation. She used nothing. She said to me later that the pain was excruciating, but she didn't want any chemical helpers to slow down the process. Fortunately for her, she has a high threshold for pain.

I stayed with Suzy the whole time, never showing a trace of anxiety. Finally, when Alec was born, I walked out in the hall and wept uncontrollably. I was not only touched that Alec was born, but that Suzy was okay, too. I probably looked worse than Suzy after Alec was born. (Cheeks said I looked like Herman Munster. You see what kind of friends I have?)

My sister and cousins were at the hospital. Their most fond memory of Alec's birth was when I came out to tell them. Instead of telling them if it was a boy or a girl, I just told them that the baby's head was as big as a hospital. "You should have seen the size of his head! It was humungous! I've never seen a baby's head that big before."

"Well, I guess he had a boy then," said my sister Chrissy. "So, you're going to name him Bighead, huh? Or maybe Hugh—short for Humongo. Or better yet—Mel—short for Melon because he's got a huge one."

I feel as if I've had everything doubly restored to me. Everything had been taken from me: my wife, my home, my health, and my future. Then, years later, it was restored back. I have a great wife, a new home, my health, a future, and my newest joy, my son Alec Robert.

Every time I look at him and Suzy, I'm so grateful that I never gave up. Otherwise, I would have never seen Alec's birth. I would have never gotten to hear him say "Da Da" for the first time, something he said way before he said mama. I would've missed out on the experience of being in a Cracker Barrel restaurant when he was one year old and seeing him make a rooster hairdo with the mashed potatoes, put peas up his nose and corn in his ears, and have chicken hanging on his face. The entire ten-foot area in every direction around his high chair looked like a battle zone. I would have missed picking him up from the high chair and walking him out the door with food dropping from inside his pants with every step he took.

Recently I was relaxing at home, sitting around in sweats and a t-shirt. Alec came up to me and innocently looked at the large prominent scar on my arm. He stared at it for a few seconds, pointed his little finger, and said, "Boo Boo." I smiled at him with tears streaming down my face and nodded, "Yes." He looked up at me with his amazing eyes, then I grabbed him and hugged him as if I had never hugged him before. I love to look at him while he sleeps. I also love to pray over him—to cover him with blankets—he brings so much joy to our hearts.

Alec is daddy's champ. He's my miracle boy. Maybe someday he'll understand. He and Suzy have brought such joy and love back into my life after my not having any for such a long time. That, I'll make sure they always understand.

"The thief cometh not, but for to steal, and to kill, and to destroy. I am come that they might have life, and that they might have it more abundantly" (John 10:10).

CHAPTER 20

TRIUMPHANT LIVING

An important principle that we must take to heart is what I call the "Ten-Second Principle."

Our lives are built on ten-second decisions. Foundations are built on or destroyed by ten-second decisions. It is vital to learn to make good choices and to put them into practice. The key is in learning how to make good ten-second choices so that, when turmoil or difficulties arise, your foundation will be strong and you will win out in the end.

Life is not fair. It will never be fair. Think about it. Is it easier to do what is right or what is wrong? Let's be honest. It's much easier to do what's wrong. We all struggle with doing the right thing. It's against human nature to do what's right. That's why it's so hard. How many times during the day do you battle against doing what's right? We don't think about that. We think about battling against doing what's wrong. It is our mission to reverse this natural tendency. We have to train ourselves to do what is against our nature. We have to establish integrity in our lives from the start.

Things in life may not always work in the way that we want them to—we can't control that. What we *can* control is our response to what happens. Wherever we are in our lives today is due to the choices that we have made throughout our lives, ten seconds at a time, choice by choice.

Some people may be saying, "I wonder what would have happened if I had taken that job in Atlanta instead of in Boston?" You made that choice, and it's natural to second guess. We will be saying "What if?" for the rest of our lives. The point is—we have to make what we feel is the best choice and live with it. If it ends up being bad, then do something to change it. Just remember to learn something from the experience.

Back in the 1960s comedian Flip Wilson used to use the expression, "The devil made me do it." It was funny, and it got laughs. But it's not true. Nobody *makes* us do anything. We choose the road we will travel. No excuses. No regrets. An excuse is a statement given for not accomplishing something. "I forgot to do it." "I'm sorry, I was too busy." "My dog ate my homework." People who have truly overcome have come to realize that excuses cannot be a part of the victory.

If a situation gets us down, we must learn to face up to it and make the best of it. I like to say, "I will do all I can possibly do, and then some." An overcomer makes a habit of working toward good decisions. It takes practice and getting into a routine. Proper practice makes perfect. Positive repetition breeds success.

Difficulties and adversity stretch us as people. People who overcome can relate to and are more understanding of those who have pain in their lives, because there is a depth in their own lives. Every person has the capacity to deal with tough situations, but it's our reaction to those hard times that shape us. A lot depends on what foundation has been built. Going through tough times and dealing with them well is known as character-building.

I like to think of each one of us as a well. At first, when we're young and inexperienced, the well is shallow. As we get older or have to take on more difficult circumstances, the well gets deeper. As the well gets deeper, its capacity to handle more grows. If we choose not to accept responsibilities or face challenges, the well doesn't change because we have not changed.

You know people all around you who have very shallow wells. They are very shallow people. You also know people who have deep wells. They are the people who have real depth to their lives. Some people are content with being shallow. Others welcome the responsibility of having depth. Here again, there is a choice. Which type of person are you?

Experiencing the tragedy brought me to a greater love and appreciation of life. Since then I have always cherished life with a true zest. Now, my love of life is greater because I have stood at death's door. Such an experience changes you. It gives you an appreciation for the simple things in life. It gives you a new perspective on how precious and short life is.

Bobby Hurley, the All-American basketball player from Duke University, was almost killed by another driver after he left the arena following a game for his professional team, the Sacramento Kings. One of the first things that Hurley talked about as he recovered from the initial surgeries was how much more he appreciated life. Life is fragile. It's brief. And it's not to be taken for granted.

Jim Valvano, the coach of the 1983 National Champion North Carolina State basketball team, died of cancer in 1993. In the winter before his death, he made an appearance at the ESPY Awards honoring excellence in athletics. Anyone who saw and heard his speech knows that it was a tremendously moving experience. Valvano, knowing that he did not have long to live, wanted to remind everyone of how precious life is and to treat it with respect. His motto that still rings in the hearts of athletes and sportscasters across the country is, "Don't give up. Don't ever give up."

Life is but a vapor. My life could have easily been taken that October night. The heartache and pain that I went through after that night allowed my personal well to become deep. I now adore every second and minute of life that I have.

Victorious people treasure life. They recognize that life will always have shortcomings and struggles. You have to climb above these things and put them under your feet. Stand on top of them and don't let them drag you down.

To live triumphantly, you want to live life to the fullest—to remember that every decision you make is of utmost importance. For every decision you make, there will always be an outcome—whether good or bad. Practice, routine, habit, balance, and priority are important components in your life. Each decision we make takes no more than ten seconds, though the outcome could have lasting effects. Each decision either strengthens or weakens our life's foundations.

Good lifestyle choices are essential to triumphant living.

CHAPTER 21

CAN I MAKE A DIFFERENCE?

People in general have problems and are looking for hope. This may not be more evident anywhere than in the lives of young people.

A combination of events started me thinking that I could make a difference in the lives of young people. The first was that assembly program at Mineola High School on Long Island, New York, exactly one year to the day after the accident happened, and the positive response that the students and faculty gave me.

The response from that program was overwhelming. From that point on, I knew that I *had* to alert young people to the dangers of drug and alcohol abuse, the importance of making good ten-second decisions, and what it means to live a triumphant life.

I had overcome so much adversity and difficulty to get to that point in my life that I wanted to share with as many people as possible so that they, too, could overcome anything that would stand in their way.

More and more, I was asked to speak to various groups and talk about what had happened. In addition to talking about the dangers of drug and alcohol abuse, I incorporated decision making, forgiveness, and overcoming into my talks.

I have a desire and burden for youth and want to touch as many people as I can. It's very clear to me now: My experience in teaching health education, coaching football, basketball, track, and baseball, working with groups such as S.A.D.D., the Fellowship of Christian Athletes, being a family life and sex education instructor, high school guidance counselor, and my educational degrees (a B.S. in HPE and master's degree in counseling), along with overcoming the tragedy, had prepared me for this next step—motivational speaking. But if you had told me five years ago that I would be doing what I am today, I would have laughed in your face. Me, a speaker?

In August and September 1991 I spent several nights wrestling with the idea of pursuing speaking on a more active level. Maybe I too could have an impact on young people's lives. Maybe I could make a difference.

Different people were instrumental in my decision to go into full-time speaking. The first, and most important person, was my wife Suzy. I felt this was something that I might like to do, but I was sensitive to how it might affect her. Suzy dispelled all my reservations.

"Bobby, you're young. You've been through a tragic situation. Look where your life is now. With the experience that you've had working with young people, I think that you'll have the possibility of really making a difference in their lives because of what you've come through. You've worked with them. You know how they think. You can encourage them by what you say and do in working with them."

Her telling me this and letting me know that she would stand by my side was a huge confirmation that this is what I should eventually do.

The second person was my friend Cheeks. Cheeks had a bachelor's degree and a master's in communication. When I started to share with him what I wanted to do, he said, "Petro, I was there with you from the beginning. And I took you aside at the funeral parlor that day when we were viewing Ava. I told you, 'Pet, I know this is going to sound stupid—and this is the craziest time to tell you this—but I really feel that God is going to someday touch millions through this tragedy."

He went on to say, "I've seen where you've come from—and where you are now. This is the most incredible story of overcoming tragedy that I have ever seen. You have to share it with others, so that they may be encouraged, too."

That was the second of three confirmations. Doors were opening for me to pursue speaking full-time.

In the fall of 1991, I returned to Great Bridge High School after working for two years as a family life sex-education specialist throughout the city of Chesapeake. I had now taken a position as high school guidance counselor. Bob Robinson had just become the principal. He was a friend of mine and while he was still the head coach had hired me in

1988 as a health education teacher and assistant football coach.

Bob knew about my story and had heard me speak on several occasions. He and the counseling department at Great Bridge encouraged me to get out and share my story with other schools around the state and in our region. Bob continued to be supportive of me even though I had to miss more and more days of school because I was getting more invitations to speak. He completely understood what I was trying to do, and allowed me to miss days to fulfill a speaking schedule that was becoming more and more demanding. Bob's encouragement and flexibility and that of several other staff at Great Bridge High School was the third confirmation that this was my new direction.

When Suzy and I were on our honeymoon cruise, we met a stand-up comedian named Stu Moss. Stu was touched by my story and encouraged me to share it more and more. He even gave me ideas about using humor in the program. Finally, when I presented this idea of speaking to family and other friends, they were all supportive.

Thanks Sharon, Mesh, and Uncle Bob. Thank you Pastor Jerry Qualls at Glad Tidings Church in Norfolk, Virginia, for your encouragement and support. You are my modern-day Pastor Greco from Brooklyn.

What I finally had to rely on was that "knowing" feeling. "I know that I know that I know that I know—that this is what I'm supposed to do."

I was going to have to rely on my faith and determination to make a difference.

CHAPTER 22

YOUTH

In my years working with people, I've been continually encouraged to focus on and target the younger generation, and I'm grateful for the opportunity to try to make a difference in their lives. My life has been dedicated to bringing a three-fold message: First, a message of faith, hope, and courage. Second, a message of the dangers of drug and alcohol abuse, which destroys lives, relationships, careers, and dreams. Such abuse is Destructive—period. Destructive with a capital "D." Third, to help young people understand the outcomes associated with ten-second decisions. They can be positive, or they can be very negative. The point is—whether they choose good or bad—they have control over which decision they want to make.

Young people are growing up faster and faster today. Physically, teenagers are way ahead of where they were just five years ago. Look at high school football and basketball players, for example. They're bigger, stronger, faster—overall better athletic specimens than before. Girls who are fourteen, fifteen, and sixteen years old today look as if they should be in their twenties.

Physically, they're mature, but emotionally they may not be.

There are always exceptions to the rule, but overall, young people today are being asked to grow up much too quickly. They're asked to act like adults before they're ready to handle such a requirement. Young people need guidance. They need discipline. Whether we believe it or not, they *want* discipline.

They also want to have boundaries and goals and to take on responsibility. Too many young people view life as if they have no responsibilities. Maturity and responsibility go hand in hand. Young people need rules to be established for them. What's more, they need these rules to be enforced. If we teach children to do what is right at an early age, it can set them on the proper course for the rest of their lives. On the other hand, if we do not teach children to do what is right at an early age, it can set them on a disastrous course for the rest of their lives.

It's true. Starting at a young age, children need to learn respect and obey authority. I'm constantly reminded of this fact by stories I hear in my travels across the country. One man told me about an incident involving his parents' home in western Pennsylvania. The neighborhood in which he grew up used to be a respectable middle-class area, one in which children played football in the street, whiffle ball in the alley, and basketball in the backyard.

"In the summertime, ten or twelve of us got together every night and played a chase game called 'Release the Den.' Now," he said, "twenty years later, I go back to the old neighborhood and feel like a stranger. It has an uncomfortable and lonely feeling. It bothers me because I have so many childhood memories, but now I hate to go back there at all.

"I would love to go back and see children riding bikes in the street and playing football. I would love to see children eight and nine years old playing 'Super heroes' and pretending to be Superman, Batman, and Spiderman—but they don't. They're too busy throwing rocks at my parents' back window. They have nothing better to do than to throw rocks at my parents' window. Respect. That's what is lacking. We were taught never to throw rocks at someone's window, whether the house was empty or not—period."

Respect. Young people need to learn it, and it's the adults who have to take the responsibility for teaching them. It's getting harder every year, but we must not back down and give up hope young people are worth the effort. They are. Unquestionably.

I want to give young people courage. I want to give them faith—faith that no matter how devastating things can be in life, no matter how dark the situation looks, no matter how difficult, and no matter how distraught they become, they can overcome it. They must overcome it. Any difficulty and adversity can be overcome.

Young people have to be taught how to establish a strong foundation. We as adults need to either reinforce and strengthen existing foundations, tear down weak or poor ones and rebuild strong ones in their place, or help those who have never had a positive foundation at all to begin building one.

Many young people today are out of control. They think that anything goes. This is the generation of "experimentation," and experimentation is becoming common in every aspect of their lives. They experimenting with sex, with drugs, with alcohol—whatever they can try that will give them a new thrill.

Teenagers today always talk about being "bored." This is the "Entertain Me" generation. Teachers today have to be part-teacher, part-motivator, and even part-entertainer. There is something to be said about creative teaching methods, but many young people don't feel a need to learn. They'd much rather be entertained than put forth the effort themselves to work hard in their studies.

Yet, perhaps the most alarming trend I see is youth "experimenting with power." This is the power of life and death. Every day there are new stories of young people killing others. For what? The thrill of power. The power to take a life. This is disturbing because there seems to be less and less value placed on human life, and we are all becoming desensitized to the violence and murder that's happening all around us. Think about it. When we watch the evening news, the top stories are usually about some horrific act against people. We see this so much it doesn't shock or affect us anymore. We're used to it. We accept it.

There must be a reversal in this. Many of us have lost our sensitivity and also our compassion. We have to start feeling again. Have we hardened ourselves so much that we don't care anymore? We can't afford to think, It happened to somebody else but not to me, so I'm not going to worry about it and maybe it'll go away. Our children learn directly from us, they watch us and observe our every move. We may not think so, but they do. If we are uncaring and apathetic adults, our children are going to follow our example and be just like we are. And that is very sad, especially when we have the power to do something about it. We need to go back to square one—back to the beginning, back to instilling strong foundations in our children. We must take the initiative and be responsible in teaching our youngsters the value of respect and having morals. No one else will do this for us. We have to make up our minds that we will do this, and then follow the Nike Principle: "Just Do It."

I challenge every parent, teacher, educator, youth pastor, anyone who works with adolescents to take five minutes a week—five minutes is all—to talk to or spend with a youngster in a one-on-one situation. I guarantee that it will make all the difference in the world. Young people today are longing for someone who really cares and loves them as they are, someone whom they can talk to and trust.

We are turning into an untrusting society and the results are obvious. We must reverse this, because with trust comes maturity, and with maturity comes responsibility, and with responsibility comes respect. That's what we need more of from all of us at every level. But it all starts with us. We adults are leaders and role models. We've got to set the standard, then abide by it so that it becomes the rule.

I wouldn't say that all of our young people are causing problems. Many more are working to do the right thing. But they are in danger of being influenced in the wrong direction. The pressures on our young people today are far greater than they were for any past generation.

Think about the importance today of image. "Image is everything," say television commercials: wear the right clothes, use the right razor, and drink the right beer. If you do these three things, you'll have a wonderful, exciting, and fulfilling life—or so they want us to believe.

Think about the casual attitudes toward sex. More and more young people are becoming sexually active at an earlier age. Elementary school children are now entering into this trend. Children are losing their innocence much too quickly. Many of them are missing out on so much of their childhood because of the pressures put on them to grow up. Teenagers think that they are adults and are ready to make adult decisions. They, too, are being cheated out of some of the best years of their lives—years that go by too quickly and can never be recovered.

Responsibility. That's what it comes down to—responsibility. They have to know that the choices they make affect not only themselves, but many others.

Young people need to have their energy focused in a positive direction. Time after time I hear stories of a teacher, a coach, or a clergyman who took the time to invest in a young person's life. Many of the most successful leaders, business people, and athletes have the same story—that someone older than them was willing to take the time to help establish good foundations in their lives. That energy, creativity, and natural ability was cultivated and given a chance to grow and mature. This is our responsibility as adults, to take the time to encourage young people in positive directions, to teach them how to make good ten-second choices that will lead them in the right direction.

I'm a firm believer that there is good in all of us. Even those who seem hardened and unreachable I believe can be reached. I don't believe that anyone is so far gone the wrong way that they cannot come back. We have to have hope. We have to believe there is always a way. Always.

I compare struggling youth to an athletic contest—an athletic contest without rules, regulations, boundaries, referees, or time clocks. Imagine the New York Giants football team playing the Buffalo Bills in the Super Bowl. It's an all-out winner-take-all game. No referees. No sidelines. No penalty flags or fifteen-yard unsportsmanlike conduct infractions. There is no forty-second clock and there are no fifteen-minute quarters. Can you imagine the confusion and hysteria that would take place? It would be total anarchy. Fans could come to the stadium and see mass chaos as they enjoyed a hot dog and soda.

This is what's happening with many of our young people today, as they get more and more out of control. They have no rules to live by, no set time they have to be in, no penalties for disobedience or disrespect. When I was growing up, I would get the belt across my behind while some of my friends would get paddled with "the board of education"—a paddle that would keep them in line.

I think many of us have become numb to deviant behavior. An editorial staff writer for a December 1993 New York *Newsday* story wrote:

> Soaring rates of illegitimacy and homelessness; drive-by shootings in drug infested neighborhoods that leave children dead in streets; guns as common in schools as bubble gum used to be. The list goes on. It's numbing. And perhaps that's at the root of the problem. We ought to be in panic.
>
> Instead, we are numb. Maybe it's the only

way to cope with it all. Gradually, Americans have become inured to the moral deterioration of society. In an untenable situation with no way out, that's an understandable response. It's also a response that leads to hopelessness, not to change. Yet, accepting immoral, deviant behavior as simply another manifestation of everyday life, with little value judgment attached to it, is exactly what we have been doing.

As Sen. Daniel Patrick Moynihan argues, we have 'defined deviancy down' as a way to cope. To keep from becoming overwhelmed by the burgeoning of social deviancy—crime, the breakup of families, drug use, homelessness—we have in effect redefined as excusable behavior social trends that we previously found repugnant. A society has an obligation to its members and its own survival, to make sure that destructive behavior has moral imperatives against it so deeply embedded that no one can uproot them or comfortably ignore them. This society is losing its moral compass again. And without it, its survival may be in doubt.

This attitude also shows up in our educational system. A recent release on January 6, 1994, by the *Associated Press*, "U.S. Schools Striving to Stem Violence," states:

Drug sniffing dogs, metal detectors, and locker room searches are becoming more common in America's schools, as educators try to curb an epidemic of violence, the National School Board Association says. Eighty-two percent of 729 school districts responding to an association said, "Violence in the schools has increased in the past five years. Clearly, violence is not confined to urban schools, but is increasingly in rural and suburban schools as well," a report on the survey said.

Though only 5 percent of the nation's school districts participated in the survey, report author Lynne Glassman called the findings very representative of America. A study released last month by Metropolitan Life said, "More than 10 percent of teachers and one quarter of their students have been victims of violence in or near their public schools. Twenty-four percent of the districts send dogs into the schools to search for drugs, most in cooperation with local police departments. Fifteen percent of the districts responding to the survey said they use metal detectors to screen for weapons—39 percent of the districts in urban areas, 10 percent suburban, and 6 percent rural. Half the school districts said students' lockers are searched."

The lack of rules, regulations, boundaries, referees, and time clocks have encouraged deviant behavior. Recently, I read a local high school newspaper in which an article discussed how the youth of today are losing sight of values:

Of the 142 students that were surveyed, 59 percent (85 students) said they had cheated on tests, while 15 percent (22) had been caught. Cheating was just one dishonest trait discussed. The survey also showed that 89 percent (126 students) lie to their parents and 78 percent (111) of the students say they usually get away with it. Students say they usually lie to their parents about where they are going or where they have been or if they drink or smoke, or if they do their homework.

Sixteen percent of the students surveyed said they would lie on an application or in person to get a job. Also, 38 percent (54) admitted to shoplifting in the past two years.

Young people do these things because they don't think that they are wrong. They learn their values from role models, their biggest influences—friends, parents, and siblings. Students said that 67 percent of their role models lie, 40 percent cheat, and 26 percent steal.

One young man interviewed had this remarkable response:

"Not all teenagers think that dishonesty is the best policy.

You know it's wrong when it makes you feel bad after you do it. Some realize that dishonest habits formed now may cause problems later in life. You have to be responsible. If you don't, you'll never grow up."

These problems are not even considered to be major problems. More focus has been placed on sex, drugs, alcohol, and violence. Sex, with the fear of the AIDS epidemic, and teenage pregnancy, are on everyone's mind. It seems our education emphasis is on having safer sex. The message is, it's okay as long as you use a condom.

The proclamation of "safe sex" is a lie. There is no such thing as safe sex. Young people are not being taught abstinence. What's wrong with abstaining from sex until marriage? What's wrong with being a virgin when you get married? What's wrong with saving yourself for that person to whom you want to give the gift that you can never take back? Let's establish strong foundations. Young people will always strive to live up to the expectations that are set for them.

Television, advertising, movies, and music are all sending mixed messages. Sexual exploitation bombards our young people. Blue jeans commercials, ads for soft drinks, fragrances, cars—they all say the same thing: you'll look satisfying, sleek, and sexy if you'll only drink... or wear... or drive... That's the key.

We are constantly being "sold" that we need things. Material things. Everyone wants to sell you the same line. There's always a new gadget, a new thingamabob, the latest thingamajig. "You have the old one—it's time for the NEW!" Young people are being taught to judge others by the size of their wallet—instead of by the integrity of their character. There is far too much emphasis on financial success and far too little on the success of being an honest, hard-working, law-abiding citizen.

Young people are being taught, "Do whatever you need to do, as long as you get ahead of the next guy. If you don't do it first, he'll do it to you. It's a dog-eat-dog world out there." You know something—it is. It always has been. It always will be. But we have to step forward and have the guts to say, "It's tough out there—it's going to be a struggle— but remember your foundations, and above all, always do what's right."

Substance abuse among our young people is on the rise

again. Just like sex, according to high school counselors with whom I've worked, substance abuse is now starting at a younger age. Some fifteen-year-olds are now already considered "recovering alcoholics and addicts." What's worse, parents today have even stated, "We know the kids are going to drink, so we would rather have them drink at our home." Other parents are saying, "We know kids are going to have sex. I'll let them do it in the next room. At least they're being supervised."

What kind of mentality is this? We know the kids are going to break the law, or be promiscuous, so we may as well accept it and help them do it in a controlled environment? Is that the message that we're sending our children? We're resigned to the fact that we can't control their behavior, so we'll give in to what we know is wrong, help them to do wrong and assist them in making poor choices? Is this the parental wisdom and knowledge that we want them to pass on to their children? What happened to our "Yes" being yes and our "No" being no? People live up to expectations.

Have we lost sight of what is right and wrong? Many of us have. We who are responsible need to return to the ideals of the past, to reimpose moral standards and constraints. Schools and families need to work more closely on this. Why is it when we talk about morals, there's a huge outcry about not mixing religion with education? It is no secret that having good morals is a strong part of being religious and having a strong faith, but good morals also means good citizenship. Good morals lead to a healthier society. Bad morals lead to social decay. Teaching the need to be responsible for one's actions is not religion-oriented. No one likes to be physically abused. No one likes to be cheated or lied to. No one likes to have things stolen from them. Teaching people to do what is right is simply moral_ not religious—education.

The importance of reimposing moral education was reiterated in the December 1993 editorial of New York *Newsday*:

> Like an engine in danger of revving itself into destruction, American society needs some sort of built-in moral governor. Yet the antidote to this malaise is simple. It's as simple as the words that used to be spoken by grandfathers in quiet

talks to their grandchildren: balancing freedom with individual responsibility for one's own actions. It's as simple as the rules that mothers used to give their children: work hard, be kind, don't take what's not yours.

We may recall the 1950s as halcyon days of social tranquillity and safety, but we wouldn't want to return to the racial hatreds and lynchings. We must agree as a society that there are some moral imperatives that must be reintroduced into public discourse. We must try to reimpose on ourselves the moral restraints we have shucked off as irrelevant. Its not too late and, perhaps, we should all follow the advice of a yellow bumper sticker glimpsed this week on a blue Volvo. In red type it said: Commit random acts of kindness.

Think of this: the heart, mind, body, and spirit of a young person is like a sponge. Whatever it soaks up, draws in, or cleans up, that's exactly what will come out when it is squeezed. If a sponge absorbs water, it won't squeeze out orange juice. If it takes in muddy water, it won't squeeze out clean water. As the expression goes: "Garbage in, garbage out. Positive in, positive out."

It's never too late to reinforce the tenets of a good foundation. With such a breakdown in families as we see today, many times schools and motivators are the only ones left to help encourage youth.

It would be nice if the family would once again become the focal point for instilling values in young people. Even though it hasn't been this way for some years, it's never too late to give people faith, to give them hope, or give them love, the love that is so desperately needed by so many youngsters. If they don't get it from us, to whom do they turn? Their peers. Their friends. The streets.

Young people are searching for answers and meaning in life. They always have and always will. Where they find these answers and this meaning is partly, if not largely, our responsibility as parents and adults. Do we want someone else to raise our children? Times have changed; our parents and grandparents would have cringed at the thought of our being raised by someone else.

What's even worse today is that children are raising children. Thus we have people without maturity or parental wisdom who are teaching youngsters their ideas of what's right and what's wrong. Two wrongs don't make a right, so why should we accept or even allow this to happen? We do because many of us aren't willing to get involved. We don't want to fight. Let somebody else take the initiative—if they start it, maybe, just maybe, I'll consider joining in. What will it take for us to realize that this is not a battle, but a war that we're fighting? Some experts say that it's already too late. Some say that the damage is irreversible. I say it's not.

Each of us needs to make that ten-second decision that will change a life forever. We need to say right here and now that we're going to stop thinking about it and *do* it.

Young people will strive toward the expectations that have been set. In my life, no one had to tell those 850 students from Santa Fe High School to rally around Coach Petrocelli when he was experiencing tragedy. No one had to tell them to pack out the church in the middle of a hurricane for the memorial service for Ava. No one had to tell them to stand in the pouring rain, with mud up to their ankles at the cemetery, to let me know how much they loved me. They knew. They did it automatically. Why? Because they were sponges who had absorbed the love that Coach Petro had for each one of them. When it was time for them to be squeezed, the love they had absorbed came out. That's all they knew to do—to give back what had saturated their hearts.

Adults need to be more in touch with young people today. We need to know where they're coming from. As a parent or educator, we need to be familiar with their likes and dislikes. By educating ourselves in what their mindsets are, we can more effectively communicate in their language and in their world. Their sense of reality is much different than ours. What music do they listen to? Who are the people they look up to? What lingo are they using? If we understand their language, we can be a part of their growth as individuals.

I'm not saying that we should try to speak as they do or dress or act as they do—No!—but we need to be current with what's happening in their lives. A big mistake would be to try to act as if we're on their level. We're not. We have to be who we are in our own generation. We dress a certain way and talk a certain way. We should never try to be something we're not. When someone is genuine and honest, you can't dispute that. People want honesty. Even if they disagree with you, they respect you for being honest. Phoniness only hurts the situation. We know when someone is being phony and when someone is being real; we can detect it. There's a mechanism inside each one of us that can sense nonverbal communication when someone is not being truthful. It's something that we just know. Young people can see right through it, too.

I personally have worked hard at keeping up with the current trends. Whether it's watching MTV and VH1 or listening to popular music stations and reading magazines that interest young people, it's all part of understanding why they think as they do. Believe me, it's work to try and stay current with what's cool today and what's not cool tomorrow, but this is what we have to do to have a greater impact on their lives. It's well worth it, but it takes work. However, the time and energy you take to research what makes them tick will pay off in the end. You'll get their respect, and that's the first step to having an effect on their lives in a positive way.

For example, one day while working as a high school counselor, I stepped out of my office and noticed a young man leaning against the wall. He had the appearance of someone into heavy metal music. How did I know? He was wearing a "Metallica" t-shirt. The day before, I had taken the time to watch MTV and had seen a Metallica music video so that I could be more up-to-date with my students' music.

I asked him if he had seen that particular music video. He looked at me and his eyes grew so big he could probably see the whole world at one time. He said, "Mr. Petro, you listen to Metallica? You listen to heavy metal music?" I had connected. I was in his world now. A bond was formed because of a ten-second decision I had made. We could now talk, and I could find out if something was troubling him.

Young people want to know the things they are dealing with are normal for teenage years. They want respect, discipline, boundaries, and guidelines. They want to know that someone cares for them as individuals, that someone is there for them to talk to, to help them to soak up all the positives in life. They need to know that life is wonderful and rewarding, just as they need to know about responsibility and consequences. They desperately desire love and people who will spend time with them. They want to show love, but sometimes don't know how. They want to learn to offer their love in the right way. They also want their emotions to be challenged in the right way.

I want to be a positive influence of love in their lives. I want to show them respect and hope. My goal is to show them the reason why it only takes ten seconds to change a life forever. Ten seconds can make a difference.

Let's not give up on young people. I believe in them. We can encourage them to accomplish anything that they want to, then they can truly live up to expectations, because they will have the tools and the maturity to do great things. Help them build their foundations ten seconds at a time. Ten seconds can change their lives forever, good or bad.

CHAPTER 23

MAKING A DIFFERENCE

I've been fortunate to have the opportunity to share my story of triumph over tragedy through television, radio, other media, and personal appearances. My favorite time is usually after I've spoken and get a chance to talk with people one on one. When I finish a speaking engagement, the question that always comes to my mind is, "Is this all worth it?" From the responses that I've gotten, I can say a resounding, "Yes!"

As I conclude my presentations, it seems that people always ask a similar question—the same one that a young girl from a rural community asked me after I spoke at her high school: "Bobby, how can you get up in front of people and share your story? How can you do it?"

I said to her, "Has this made a difference in your thinking? Will this possibly make a difference in your life?"

Through tear-filled eyes she said, "Yes, it has. You're a real person with real scars, pain, and triumph. Not just a video or someone we read about—but a *real person* we could see and talk to."

I'll never forget her face as I felt the sincerity in her voice. "That's why I do it. That's why I can get up in front of people and share my story," I told her.

The greatest reward is not some type of prestige or recognition. It's the lives that are touched. It's for times such as when I traveled to a college in Pennsylvania and spoke to three thousand students. At the end of the program, a female sophomore came up to talk to me. She introduced herself and said, "Bobby, you don't know me, but you have touched my life dramatically. Several years ago, while I was a senior in high school, you spoke to our student body. I was there with my closest group of friends. We were some of the biggest 'partyers' and drinkers in the school. You didn't know this until now, but after you spoke, my friends and I were really touched. You made such a strong impact on our lives that when I told my friends you were coming here to my college, they were excited and relived the time you spoke at our high school. We discussed how your message from two years ago still has a positive influence on us today."

Recently, after I completed a program at a school in Connecticut, the school's social worker approached me and immediately began to open up. She explained how her life had been devastated because of her ex-husband's cocaine habit. She said she was exhausted physically, mentally, spiritually, and financially. I could tell that she was becoming emotional. As she slowly walked away, full of tearful emotion, she said, "You have brought me something that I have needed so desperately. You have brought me hope."

While speaking recently in New York, I was encouraged by a school psychologist. She wanted to introduce me to a student with whom she had been working. After I met this student in a casual manner, the psychologist and I stepped into her office. She said to me, "You have had a major impact on the life of that young boy. Recently, he got into a legal problem. While drunk, he and several other students beat up a younger, defenseless student. They beat him up so badly they sent him to the hospital. When I met with him after your program, he was in tears. He now realized, more than ever, how much his ten-second decision had changed his life and hurt this other boy. He was seeking to get comfort and help, and I guess to find forgiveness. He experienced that in your story."

I'm reminded of a young girl in Virginia who approached me at the end of an assembly at her school. This was the third assembly at this particular school, in which I shared with more than two thousand students. She came running to me, weeping and sobbing. She said, "Bobby, I'm seventeen years old. Since I was fourteen, my parents have placed me in several detention homes and other foster homes because I was incorrigible. For four years I have bounced from home to home, leaving nothing but a path of problems in my wake. I've talked to my parents, counselors, social workers, and psychologists but, for some reason, no one has ever been able to get through to me. You are the first person to break through and to make sense. Everything that everyone has ever shared with me has finally hit home because of things you have shared. I really realize how much I want to better my life."

Many times I've had the opportunity to speak at school-sponsored evening programs. I finished speaking at a rural town in North Carolina where about two hundred students, parents, teachers, and administrators were in attendance. At the end of the presentation, an older couple came up to me.

"Bobby," the older gentleman called to me from thirty feet across the auditorium. He and his wife walked slowly toward me and I could see that they were in their late sixties.

"Thank you, Bobby," he said as the tears welled up in his eyes.

"Yes. Thank you, Bobby," his wife said in a frail and cracking voice.

I looked into their teary eyes and saw a world of sadness and hurt. Just seeing the depth of the pain in their faces caused a rush of emotion inside me that I'll never forget. I can't recall ever trying so hard not to lose my composure than that night after speaking to this particular group.

"Our son was only thirty-nine years old when he was killed two years ago by a drunk driver."

It was at that moment I knew why I had become so emotional at simply seeing the hurt in their faces. Something in my heart had identified with the grief they experienced in losing their son as I had lost Ava.

"Our boy was a good boy. He never done nothin' to hurt nobody. He always went to church, had a good job, took care of his wife, and had five beautiful children," the man said before he was overcome with tears. He stepped forward and I wrapped my arms around both him and his wife. They wept openly for several minutes. I wanted to, but I held it inside—to this day I don't know why.

"My son and I were very close, you see. Very close," he said in a choked, whispering voice. "We're a God-fearing family and we believe that there's always a reason for whatever happens to us in life. But this—this was hard for us to accept. Very hard for us to accept," he said, fighting to be strong in the face of such a painful admission. "We want to thank you for coming here tonight to our little school and sharing what happened to your wife. In a strange way, we feel that there is someone else in the world who knows a little bit how we feel."

At that instant I couldn't hold back any longer and the tears welled in my eyes. I began to sweat because the compassion and understanding I felt from that older couple was like nothing I had felt before. Here was a couple who had gone through a loss similar to mine. They knew firsthand the frustration, the anger, the helplessness, and the loneliness of losing someone so dear.

"You don't know how much you touched us," the woman said.

"Thank you, Bobby," the man repeated again. "You just don't know how much your coming here has meant to us."

I hugged and kissed them and thanked them for encouraging me that night. As they turned and walked away into the shadows of the auditorium and out into the night, I thought to myself, "You'll never know how much you've touched me, Bobby Petrocelli, here tonight."

I stood there alone in the auditorium as the janitor took down the microphone and swept up the aisle. I can still see their faces. I can still hear their voices. I can still hear the echoes—they never knew how much they touched me that night in that little school in North Carolina. This is why I do it. For the rare moments like these.

Success is something we should all strive for. It's measured in different ways. Some would say that success is measured in what you have monetarily. Others would say that success is measured in the stature that you attain as an individual, an athlete, a business person, a movie star, a politician, etc. To reach a certain goal or plateau is something to strive for—but what do we do with that position once we've attained it?

To me, a successful person is one who touches others' lives in a positive way. It doesn't matter what you choose to pursue in life—being a good housewife, a janitor, winning the World Series, being the president of the United States— whatever. Is your goal to gain prestige for yourself, or to serve others?

One final story was shared with me as a young boy and has stayed with me throughout my life:

Several people had passed from this life and were now standing in the presence of God in Heaven. They stood there looking at mansion after mansion throughout Heaven.

Gorgeous, spectacular, breathtaking, indescribable—words could not articulate the beauty of the gold and diamonds that shimmered in the radiance of the brightness there.

As God showed each one their mansion, they came upon the most beautiful one of all. It was on a hillside and radiated with a glow of beauty around it. The first person said, "Oh, this must be the mansion of _____ , the person who worked so hard to tell people about God, clothe the hungry, and feed the poor."

Everyone else agreed and whispered among themselves. God looked at them all with a smile on His face and said, "No, this is not the mansion of _____ , who served those you described, but of the one who gave of his time, his money, and his prayers so that the other person could accomplish all that was necessary to help people in need."

Serving people in love is one of the greatest gifts we can give. I believe that in saving, helping, or giving hope to one, we are helping the world. I travel and speak wherever I can—and to whomever I can—so that those who are willing to listen may know that they can also triumph. You have to choose to do it. I did. And so can you. You can make a difference. You too can triumph over any tragedy.

When my life on earth is over—when I've shared my last story, tried to motivate and inspire that last person—I want to know that my actions truly spoke louder than my words. The words that I'll desire to hear most are, "Well done, thou good and faithful servant" (Matthew 25:21).

EPILOGUE

Now that you know the whole story, are you wondering about how to implement the details of a victory over tragedy? Each of us faces uncontrollable situations, though we all have dominion over how we respond to each one. Everyday decisions are not insignificant, they are essential to our lives.

The determinant is our actions. It only takes ten seconds to make a difference. As we continue to add seconds, we eventually reach a minute, an hour, a day, a week, a month, and a lifetime. Remember the quote, "Even Rome was not built in a day." Patterns, routines, and habits are formed one by one. We build our foundation one brick (decision, choice) at a time, a foundation that can weather the elements of life. There's no quick fix. It takes hard work and commitment (something that has lost its popularity in our society). Many blame God or others for misfortune. We all have the greatest God-given gift of all, a free will. Whatever it may take, get the ball rolling. Move things in a positive direction.

Focus on an area of interest and get involved. Do whatever is possible to aid someone else. I've used the sayings, "Save one and you save the world," and, "When you help someone in need, you are also helping yourself." Let's center on serving others who are in similar or even more difficult circumstances. Not only will you be doing something positive, but you'll probably feel a lot better about yourself.

Life many times has been described as a rollercoaster ride. There are two types of people on that rollercoaster: One holds on for dear life, while the other lets go, throws his arms up, and allows himself to go along for the ride. Which type of person are you?

Friend, my ultimate desire is that you find faith, hope, and love.

APPENDIX

QUOTES TO LIVE BY

"You will be in a great position to have health
and success if your relationship with God,
your Source, is right."
—Oral Roberts

"It is impossible to accomplish anything worthwhile
without the help of others."
—Unknown

"Good and Evil increase at compound interest.
That is why the little decisions you and I make
every day are of such infinite importance."
—C.S. Lewis

"It's not what happens to you,
it's what you do about it."
—W Mitchell

"The will to win is important,
but the will to prepare is vital."
—Joe Paterno

"I've learned that if you keep doing what
you've always done, you'll keep getting
what you've always gotten."
—Unknown

"No one is immune from feelings of injustice.
Life's not fair, but let's not mix up life
with God. God is not the source of injustice.
God is fair. God is good."
—Robert H. Schuller

"I have learned that success is to be measured
not so much by the position that one has reached
in life, as by the obstacles which he has
overcome while trying to succeed."
—Booker T. Washington

"Nothing splendid has ever been achieved
except by those who believed that something inside
of them was superior to circumstances."
—Bruce Barton

"I've learned that every great achievement
was once considered impossible."
—Unknown